eight sessions for
a children's club

© Sue Clutterham 2005
First published 2005

ISBN 1 84427 153 6

Scripture Union, 207–209 Queensway, Bletchley, Milton Keynes, MK2 2EB, United Kingdom
Email: info@scriptureunion.org.uk
Website: www.scriptureunion.org.uk

Scripture Union Australia, Locked Bag 2, Central Coast Business Centre, NSW 2252, Australia
Website: www.scriptureunion.org.au

Scripture Union USA, PO Box 987, Valley Forge, PA 19482, USA
Website: www.scriptureunion.org

All rights reserved. No part of this publication may be reproduced, stored in a retrieval system, or transmitted in any form or by any means, electronic, mechanical, photocopying, recording or otherwise, without the prior permission of Scripture Union.

Pages 19 to 27 may be photocopied in the context of using *Awesome!*

The right of Sue Clutterham to be identified as the author of this work has been asserted by her in accordance with the Copyright, Designs and Patents Act 1998.

Scripture quotations are from the Contemporary English Version © American Bible Society 1991, 1992, 1995. Anglicisations © British and Foreign Bible Society 1997, published in the UK by HarperCollins*Publishers*. Used by permission.

British Library Cataloguing-in-Publication Data.
A catalogue record of this book is available from the British Library.

Printed and bound in Malta by Interprint.
Illustration by Colin Smithson.
Cover and internal template design by Kevin Wade of kwgraphicdesign.

Thanks to the leaders of the following midweek clubs who tried out this material and sent loads of suggestions to make this programme even better!

The Hothouse, Aldridge, W Midlands; **Storykeepers Club**, North Cheam Baptist Church, Surrey; **2nd Croxley Green Girls' Brigade**, Rickmansworth; **Garthamlock Primary SU Group**, Glasgow; **Way in Primary Club**, Gorgie, Edinburgh; **Kidz Klub**, Page Moss, Liverpool; **Jzone**, Cheam Park Farm Junior School, Sutton, Surrey; **21st Cardiff Boys' Brigade**, Ararat Baptist Church, Cardiff.

Awesome! is an *eye level* club programme, part of *eye level*, Scripture Union's project to catch up with children and young people who have yet to catch sight of Jesus.

Scripture Union is an international Christian charity working with churches in more than 130 countries, providing resources to bring the good news of Jesus Christ to children, young people and families and to encourage them to develop spiritually through the Bible and prayer.

As well as our network of volunteers, staff and associates who run holidays, church-based events and school Christian groups, we produce a wide range of publications and support those who use our resources through training programmes.

Contents

Starting out — **6**
- How to use *Awesome!* — 6
- Getting to know you — 8
- Working with small groups — 9
- Helping children respond — 10
- What to do after *Awesome!* — 11
- Extra activities — 12
- *Awesome!* banner — 13
- The book of John – Bible text — 14
- 'God is an awesome God' – OHP words — 19
- 'God is an awesome God' – sheet music — 20
- Photocopiable resources — 22

Jesus has God's power — **29**

Jesus can do the impossible — **34**

Jesus knows what's best for us — **38**

Jesus cares for us in ways that matter — **42**

Jesus helps us understand God — **46**

Jesus gives new life — **50**

Jesus is alive for ever! — **54**

What about us? — **58**

Other resources — **62**

Starting out

How to use Awesome!

Jesus, the amazing, miracle-working Son of God, wants us to be his friends. Awesome! *Awesome!* unwraps the miracles of Jesus recorded in John's Gospel as signs that point to Jesus as the Son of God. The material is suitable for use in a midweek club, weekend event or school Christian group.

The aim of Awesome!

The aim is to help everyone meet Jesus, and respond in amazement at who he is and what he has done. The activities make very few assumptions about children's previous knowledge of the Bible or experience of a Christian community. There is plenty of scope for relationship building – with each other and God.

At the heart of *Awesome!* is the intention that children have fun as they build relationships with other children and adult leaders. In this context, leaders can naturally share Jesus and what he means to them. Over the weeks trust will grow, as will the questions children ask and the answers they find. Our hope is that the Holy Spirit will be at work in the life of each child who attends, whether this is the first time they have been part of anything Christian or they are already part of a church community.

How the programme works

This eight-week programme is designed to go with the *Awesome!* DVD – seven five-minute illustrated stories that focus on the miracles of Jesus recorded in John's Gospel. The material was originally produced as the *Signposts* video, which is still available from SU Mail Order or your local Christian bookshop. The DVD contains the *Awesome!* song and additional resources.

The *Awesome!* song on page 19 was written specifically for the club. It is available on the CD *Light for Everyone* (£9.99, 1 84427 080 7, SCRIPTCD 01), which also contains non-confessional songs ideal for use if you have children in your group not connected to a church. *Light for Everyone* also includes a CD-ROM of song words and sheet music. The *Awesome!* song is also available on the *Awesome!* DVD.

Each session is divided into three parts – *Eye openers*, *Fact finders* and *Sign spotters*. Choose some or all of the activities on offer in each part. The times in brackets for each activity indicate how long to allow whether you're running a short session that lasts half an hour, or a longer session that runs for an hour and a half or more. But do recognise that the unique nature of your group means these timings are not 100 per cent applicable.

> If you don't have access to a DVD player, the material is also available in video format as the *Signposts* video. This is available from SU Mail Order or from your local Christian bookshop.

What's in the programme

Each miracle was a sign that pointed to Jesus as the Son of God. The *Awesome!* DVD condenses the fourth and fifth signs (the feeding of the 5,000 and Jesus walking on the water) into one sequence and includes the ultimate miracle of Jesus' resurrection as the seventh sign. There are eight *Awesome!* session outlines altogether - the final session summarises the whole series:

- Sign 1: 'Jesus has God's power' John 2:1–11 (Jesus turns water into wine)
- Sign 2: 'Jesus can do the impossible' John 4:46–54 (Jesus heals an official's son)
- Sign 3: 'Jesus knows what's best for us' John 5:1–18 (Jesus heals the man by the pool)
- Sign 4: 'Jesus cares for us in ways that matter' John 6:1–21 (Jesus feeds 5,000 people)
- Sign 5: 'Jesus helps us understand God'

John 9:1–38 (Jesus heals a blind man)
- Sign 6: 'Jesus gives new life' John 11:1–44 (Jesus raises Lazarus from the dead)
- Sign 7: 'Jesus is alive for ever!' John 20:1–18; 21:1–14 (Jesus is raised to life)
- Final sign-up: What about us? John 20:30,31

 Part 1: Eye openers
(5–20 minutes)

Eye openers is a selection of fun activities that introduce the session's theme. They involve movement, games, refreshments and action – a good way for everyone to get to know each other better and let off steam at the beginning of a session. Vary the time according to the mood of the children as they arrive, the type of venue you have, the number of helpers and the time available for your session.

If your group is meeting straight after school, the children may need to run around and let off steam or they may be just tired out! They will certainly need refreshments. After their evening meal they will be more relaxed. On Saturday or Sunday they will be different again. You will have to assess what best introduces them to the *Awesome!* atmosphere. However, don't let this part of the programme go on too long. Allow enough time for *Fact finders* and *Sign spotters*.

Ideas for those first few minutes or whenever you might have a bit of extra time are on pages 12 and 13. Whatever you do, make sure that the group feels properly welcomed and comfortable.

 Part 2: Fact finders
(10 minutes)

Fact finders focuses on each session's theme in detail. Look at the *Awesome!* DVD clip and read the Bible verses with the children, then choose from a range of activities in *Sign spotters* to develop the theme.

Remember that some children find reading hard or just don't like it. Reading the Bible may appear hard work or boring, but it doesn't have to be. After all, this is God's unique Word to us. Children can listen to it being read, they can act it out, draw it, memorise it, set it to music, pick out key words and so on. Bible reading is deliberately central to this programme. That is why the Bible passages are included (see pages 14–18) so that you can put them on an OHP acetate or reproduce them if you want to. The Bible could be part of a child's life, long after you have left them! So be imaginative in how you use it. Your enthusiasm for God's Word will be infectious.

The Bible verses have been reproduced from the Contemporary English Version and used with permission. This version is especially good for reading out loud. But whatever version of the Bible you use, make sure it is child-friendly and doesn't look old or out of date!

 Part 3: Sign spotters
(15–60 minutes)

Sign spotters suggests activities to consolidate the learning. Select activities according to the size of the group, the ages of the children and the help you have available.

Make sure that you end properly and as calmly as possible. Try to say goodbye to each child personally. The children will be more likely then to remember what they have learnt and be aware of the positive relationships there have been in *Awesome!* Friendships made with other children and leaders may be the most important part of *Awesome!*

Eight midweek clubs tested the *Awesome!* programme. Their comments and experience have helped to shape the published programme. Some of the comments have been printed for your inspiration.

> Catch up with other *Awesome!* users on the eye level website! Register your club and download PDFs of the photocopiable pages: www.scriptureunion.org.uk/eyelevel

 Awesome reminder!

Awesome! sessions work as single sessions but are designed to be part of a programme. To help the children be aware of this and make connections from one week to the next, you could create a simple display. Put the word 'Awesome!' onto A4 paper and each week stick it to the centre of a noticeboard in the room or hall where you meet. Add any artwork that the children have done each week. In a church, the display could stay for the duration of the programme and prompt the rest of the church to pray! Alternatively, create a large banner which you add to as you progress through the programme (see page 13).

We put up the teaching points from the previous weeks which we use to recap and then add this week's point.
Rosey, North Cheam

Getting to know you…

Building relationships

The children you'll meet at *Awesome!* live in a fast-moving, sophisticated, technology-orientated world, dominated by screens. There is so much 'stuff' demanding their attention. Rather than trying to compete with that sort of environment, offer them what they are often missing elsewhere – real communication. Concentrate on the unique opportunity you have to build relationships, listen to them, talk with them, and give them time as you show them God's love in action. That way they will get to know you, each other and Jesus as they take part, and have a great time too!

Top tips for sharing Jesus with children

- Build strong friendships. Be genuinely interested in their lives, homes, interests, what happens at school. These friendships will be bridges across which Jesus can walk! Ensure that these children know that you appreciate and respect them.
- Be informed about what is happening at school and home – it's useful to be in the know about sports days, class excursions or family events, and these may explain why the children are excited or tired, or both!
- Get to know the children's families: understand their home lives, and help their parents (or whoever is responsible for their care) know what they are learning. Children can never be divorced from their home backgrounds. Avoid talking about Mum and Dad. It's best to refer to Mum or Dad or even, 'whoever looks after you at home'.
- Remember birthdays, or ask someone else to take on the responsibility of noting dates and preparing cards, perhaps for the other children to sign.
- Do as you say! The children need to see you model what you teach them. Your friendship with Jesus matters. How else will the children see what it means in practice to be in a relationship with him?
- Encourage everyone to join in – adults and children alike. Create a 'we're in this together' feel to the sessions, rather than 'them and us' – avoid organising activities that adults stand and watch. Relax, have fun and learn with the children – '…aim to give children the best hour of their week!' (Dave Connelly, Frontline Church)
- Mind your language! Avoid jargon words (eg sin, grace or churchy words) and explain what you mean by things like prayer.
- Use illustrations from everyday life to explain concepts. Jesus taught complex truths in simple ways (eg you can't see wind, but you can see the effects that it has; it's the same with the Holy Spirit). You will need to think about this before the club begins.
- Grow confidence with the Bible and explain how to read it. Why don't we often start at page 1? How do we use the contents page? (Younger children find this very hard.) What are the differences between chapters and verses, or the Old and New Testaments? How do you explain that the Bible is one big story – God's story – in different bits? Find out more about the Bible in *The Story of the Book* (see the bottom of the page).
- Talk about Jesus, rather than God, where possible. The Gospels give us clear pictures of what he is like and these are far easier to grasp than the idea of God being 'up there' but invisible. Children have some very woolly ideas about God, but there is less room for manoeuvre when it comes to Jesus!
- Apply the Bible teaching appropriately. Help them see that Jesus is alive today and is relevant to their lives.
- Allow children to make responses that are appropriate for them, their understanding and their backgrounds. Don't rush straight in with, 'Do you want to follow Jesus?' That should be a decision that lasts for life, and they need to recognise what it entails. For many children, there are a number of commitments as their understanding grows.
- Have fun together! The children need to catch something of the 'life in all its fullness' that Jesus spoke about.

The Story of the Book
Terence Copley
£8.99 1 84427 131 5

Find out more about the Bible: who wrote it? How was it put together? What is its future? These difficult questions and more are answered in a down-to-earth style in this 'unstuffy' book about God's Word.

Working with small groups

🙂 Practicalities

- Children are all different. Respect their differences.
- Make sure any child with a special need is catered for.
- Make sure children know they can come to you with any questions.
- Make sure that children are comfortable. Cold, hard floors do not encourage positive discussion. Cushions, mats or comfortable chairs can make all the difference. Sometimes, everyone lying on their tummies in a star shape can create a fantastic atmosphere – their teacher at school is unlikely to do this.
- Keep good eye contact with every child.
- In the group, watch out for children who are on the edge.
- Don't talk down to children – talk with them. This means getting to their level, physically and verbally.
- Don't always rush to fill silences while children are thinking of responses.
- Validate all responses, either by a further question or ask others what they think, especially if you don't agree with the initial comment or answer.
- If lots of children want to talk, pass an object round – only the child holding the object can speak.
- Encourage children to listen to each other (something they might find quite difficult).
- Be prepared to admit that you don't know the answer to a question, but say that you'll find out the answer, if appropriate.

🙂 Asking questions

In each session, there is a section on questions that you might ask in any group time you have, which will help the children to engage with the Bible story. Leading a small group is one of the most difficult things a children's worker has to do. Don't use all these questions as they are written. Put them into your own words. They are simply a guide for you. The questions have sometimes been incorporated into a quiz.

Ever thought about the kinds of questions you ask people? The same question can be asked in many different ways, and force the person being asked the question to give certain kinds of answers.

?? Rhetorical

If you ask, 'Isn't it great to have ice cream?', it is a rhetorical question, implying the expected answer. It brings out the right answer for the benefit of others.

?? Closed

If you ask, 'Do you like coming to *Awesome!*?', it is a closed question, mainly allowing for 'Yes' or 'No'. It encourages contributions and assesses what the children think.

?? Factual

If you ask, 'What message did the sisters send to Jesus?', it is a factual question, requiring basic information. It encourages contributions and establishes the facts.

?? Open

If you ask, 'Why did Jesus wait before going to Lazarus' house?', it is an open question, allowing broad expression. It encourages discussion and indicates what the children think.

?? Experience

If you ask, 'How would you feel if that happened to you?', it is an experience question, for sharing views or feelings. It encourages discussion and helps children to apply the teaching personally.

?? Leading

If you ask, 'What have you learnt at *Awesome!*, David?', it is a leading question aimed at getting a specific answer from someone. It indicates learning and understanding and encourages contributions.

Think about when you might use these types of questions in your group. Go through each question with your team and decide when it is appropriate and when it is inappropriate to use certain kinds of questions.

Helping children to respond

😊 Being Jesus' friend

Awesome! introduces children to people who met Jesus and got to know him. They'll also meet people in the 21st century who know and love Jesus. This may prompt children to want to be friends with Jesus for themselves. Be ready to help them.

- They rarely need long explanations, just simple answers to questions.
- Talk to them in a place where you can be seen by others.
- Never put pressure on children to respond in a particular way, just help them take one step closer to Jesus when they are ready. We don't want them to respond just to please us!
- Remember, for many children there are a number of commitments as their understanding grows.
- Many children just need a bit of help to say what they want to say to God. Here is a suggested prayer they could use to make a commitment to Jesus:

> Dear God,
> Thank you that you love me.
> I'm sorry for all the things I've done wrong, which you do not want me to do.
> Thank you that Jesus your Son came to live on earth and understands what it's like to be a child.
> Thank you that he died on the cross for me and that means I can be forgiven.
> Please forgive me.
> Please be my friend and help me each day to please you.
> Amen.

Reassure them that God hears us when we talk with him and has promised to forgive us and help us be his friends.

😊 What next?

Children need help to stick with Jesus, especially if their parents don't believe.

- Assure them that God wants them to talk with him, whatever they want to say. Give them some prayer ideas.
- Encourage them to keep coming to Christian activities, not necessarily on Sundays – their church might have to be the midweek club or a school lunch-time club.
- Reading the Bible will be easier with something like *Snapshots* – but you need to support them if they are to keep it up.
- Keep praying and maintain your relationship with them wherever possible.

😊 Some booklets that may help

Friends with Jesus
A booklet explaining what it means to make a commitment to follow Jesus for under-8s.
Single £0.99 1 84427 141 2
Pack of 20 £15.00 1 84427 144 7

Me and Jesus
A booklet explaining what it means to make a commitment to follow Jesus for 8 to 10s.
Single £0.99 1 84427 142 0
Pack of 20 £15.00 1 84427 145 5

Jesus=friendship forever
A booklet explaining what it means to make a commitment to follow Jesus for 10 to 12s.
Single £0.99 1 84427 143 9
Pack of 20 £15.00 1 84427 146 3

What Jesus did
D Abrahall
A book exploring Jesus, ideal for those with special needs.
Single £2.00 1 84427 005 X
Pack of 5 with teachers' guide £8.00 1 84427 006 8

Snapshots
Bible reading for 8- to 10-year-olds.
£2.50 single copy
£9.00 annual subscription (UK)
(Packs of 6 are also available, priced £12.50.)

(Prices are correct at the time of going to press.)

For a simple commitment card, visit the *eye level* website: www.scriptureunion.org.uk/eyelevel

What to do after Awesome!

 Step one – time to think

Hopefully *Awesome!* has made you think about how you run activities and reach out to children in your community. Before the end of the *Awesome!* series, plan a review with anyone who helped. Be as honest as you can and dream dreams!
- What did the children enjoy about *Awesome!*?
- What was different compared to your previous activities for children?
- Were there more small-group activities? How did they work?
- Was there more Bible input than before?
- What worked really well or didn't work?
- What did the leaders enjoy?
- What did you discover about each other's gifts for working with children? Was there an unknown storyteller or someone especially good at welcoming children?

Write down the most important answers. Talk about what you should do next.

 Step two – moving on

Don't be afraid to develop what you provide for children. If *Awesome!* encouraged you to run a midweek or Saturday club for the first time and it worked, plan to carry on. You may need extra help, especially if some people can't commit themselves weekly. Perhaps you could do another eight-week club next term or maybe a monthly Saturday/Sunday special, using another Scripture Union programme.

Discuss how you might contact new children. What are your links with the local school(s) or neighbourhood groups? Could you publicise your group through the local paper or library? How could the children who already come be encouraged to bring their friends? Just how many more children can you cope with?

 Step three – building on Awesome!

One of the aims of *Awesome!* is to bring children who don't usually have much contact with a Christian community into a Christian activity. If this worked for you, build on the final *Awesome!* session and get to know the children's families by running a parents' special event. Family games work well, either games to play as families or everyone all together. Any family activity that offers food will be popular! Alternatively, some churches have explored parenting groups. In one place a church football team has developed from fathers of children who started coming to a church children's club. Be imaginative and find out what other churches have done in your area. Maybe you could do something together.

Whatever you do, it is good to maintain contact with children, to sustain and grow your relationships. You may wish to visit the children. If you do so, contact the parents to make sure they are happy for you to come and to arrange a time for your visit. Visiting the children also enables you to have contact with their parents.

 Coming soon

Look out for *Landlubbers*, a holiday club programme out now, and *Clues2Use – Landlubbers on the Jesus Quest*, a follow-up programme for midweek groups. *Landlubbers* takes pirates as its theme and explores what Paul has to say through his letter to the Philippians. As with any SU programme, each day's session is packed with exciting, Bible-focused activities and is full of fun. There is an accompanying DVD and *Landlubbers Logbook*, containing the text of Philippians and loads of activities and puzzles to be used in small groups.

Clues2Use allows you to follow up your holiday club through the rest of the year. (It can be used on its own, even if you have not run the holiday club programme.) The eight-sessions follow the same pirate theme, as Landlubbers look for Jesus in the 21st century. Using *The Jesus Quest*, the Jesus Film for children distributed by Agape and SU, *Clues2Use* is designed for children who have had little or no contact with the church. For more details, see pages 62 and 63.

Streetwise, an eight-session programme similar in aim and design to *Awesome!* is already available. With an accompanying DVD (based on the *Luke Street* video), *Streetwise* introduces children to the inhabitants of various houses Jesus visited, using Luke's Gospel.

Extra activities

The first and last few minutes of a club can be the most important! Your first conversation with a child helps to settle them, for them to be open to God. You represent Jesus: your welcome is his welcome. The end of the club may be what they remember most, so make the most of the time.

A few guidelines

- Choose the right opening question for the right day: if it's the weekend, keep school conversation to a minimum.
- Be led by the child. Don't probe where they don't want to talk.
- Allow a conversation to develop rather than just asking questions.
- Help others join in as they join the group.
- Tell the children about your day to build friendships and make it less like a grilling.

Questions about school
What was the best thing that happened? Did anything funny happen? What did you have for dinner? What's the food like at your school?

General questions
What have you seen on television/read/done recently? What are you doing this weekend? How's your football team doing? Tell me about your family/what you do in your spare time.

Ideas to end the club

A routine pattern to the end may be useful.

In groups
- Chat about what they will do at home/later/during the week.
- A quick recap of the Bible teaching to help them remember/apply it.
- Pray for the week ahead.

Together
- Recap the Bible teaching and allow a moment to think about it again.
- Sit around a candle and remind them that Jesus, the light of the world, is always with us. Ask for things to pray about, or read prayers they have written during the session. (You could light the candle if you have assessed the risks and can do so safely.)
- Sing the *Awesome!* song.

Time-fillers

1. Turn everyone's name round and enjoy the different sounds! (Nhoj Htims, Enna Senoj)
2. I Spy. For very young children play 'I spy with my colour eye', with objects of a certain colour.
3. Who can… wiggle their ears, touch their nose with their tongue, recite the alphabet backwards, wiggle their eyebrows and so on.
4. Dice games: have ready-made cards with questions to be answered when the numbers are rolled.
   For example:
   Favourites: 1 – food; 2 – pop group; 3 – team; 4 – TV programme; 5 – story; 6 – colour
   Home: 1 – family; 2 – rooms; 3 – pets; 4 – food; 5 – outside the house; 6 – favourite room
   Favourite food: 1 – sandwich; 2 – drink; 3 – breakfast; 4 – biscuits; 5 – snack; 6 – worst food
5. Simon Says.
6. 'I went to spot a sign and I saw…' Each person recites the growing list and adds an item.
7. Mime things you do at home – others must guess, eg watching TV, turning on a tap.
8. Challenge the group to make a human sculpture of household objects, eg a chair, knife and fork, clock, bathroom.

If the children turn up in dribs and drabs, you may want to have a general activity that they can join in as they arrive (see page 13). Or you might want to have an ongoing activity, which the children can do as a group craft during *Sign spotters*.

Group activity

😊 Awesome! banner

What you need
- A long roll of paper, or several large sheets of paper stuck together
- Felt-tip pens
- Collage materials such as scraps of material, newspaper to tear, coloured tissue paper
- Scissors
- Glue and spreaders
- A4 paper for individual pictures
- Photos of the *Awesome!* crowd and *Awesome!* activities (optional – remember to get permission from parents)
- Other art materials (optional)

What you do
At the beginning of Session 1, challenge everyone to see if they can make a really massive *Awesome!* banner or poster. Provide materials from the list above, as appropriate. If you use a roll of paper, you could do a section each session and use a different medium for each one. Decide with the children and adult helpers on the content of each section. If possible use the 'Signs' for each session as slogans on your banner. Display the finished result at the final session. If possible, display it in your church and use it as an opportunity to tell everyone what the children have been doing at *Awesome!*

The book of John

These Bible verses for *Awesome!* are taken from the Contemporary English Version and are used with permission.

Pages 19 to 27 are photocopiable. You may photocopy any of these pages for use in your *Awesome!* programme. These pages are also available on the *Awesome!* website: www.scriptureunion.org.uk/eyelevel

 Sign 1: Jesus has God's power

John 2:1–11

Three days later Mary, the mother of Jesus, was at a wedding feast in the village of Cana in Galilee. Jesus and his disciples had also been invited and were there.

When the wine was all gone, Mary said to Jesus, "They don't have any more wine."

Jesus replied, "Mother, my time hasn't yet come! You must not tell me what to do."

Mary then said to the servants, "Do whatever Jesus tells you to do."

At the feast there were six stone water jars that were used by the people for washing themselves in the way that their religion said they must. Each jar held about a hundred litres. Jesus told the servants to fill them to the top with water. Then after the jars had been filled, he said, "Now take some water and give it to the man in charge of the feast."

The servants did as Jesus told them, and the man in charge drank some of the water that had now turned into wine. He did not know where the wine had come from, but the servants did. He called the bridegroom over and said, "The best wine is always served first. Then after the guests have had plenty, the other wine is served. But you have kept the best until last!"

This was Jesus' first miracle, and he did it in the village of Cana in Galilee. There Jesus showed his glory, and his disciples put their faith in him.

 Sign 2: Jesus can do the impossible

John 4:46–54

While Jesus was in Galilee, he returned to the village of Cana, where he had turned the water into wine. There was an official in Capernaum whose son was sick. And when the man heard that Jesus had come from Judea, he went and begged him to keep his son from dying.

Jesus told the official, "You won't have faith unless you see miracles and wonders!" The man replied, "Lord, please come before my son dies!"

Jesus then said, "Your son will live. Go on home to him." The man believed Jesus and set off to return home.

Some of the official's servants met him along the road and told him, "Your son is better!" He asked them when the boy got better, and they answered, "The fever left him yesterday at one o'clock."

The boy's father realized that at one o'clock the day before, Jesus had told him, "Your son will live!" So the man and everyone in his family put their faith in Jesus.

This was the second miracle that Jesus performed after he left Judea and went to Galilee.

Sign 3: Jesus knows what's best for us

John 5:1–18

Later, Jesus went to Jerusalem for another Jewish festival. In the city near the sheep gate was a pool with five porches, and its name in Hebrew was Bethzatha.

Many sick, blind, lame, and crippled people were lying close to the pool.

Beside the pool was a man who had been sick for thirty-eight years. When Jesus saw the man and realized that he had been crippled for a long time, he asked him, "Do you want to be healed?"

The man answered, "Lord, I don't have anyone to put me in the pool when the water is stirred up. I try to get in, but someone else always gets there first."

Jesus told him, "Pick up your mat and walk!" At once the man was healed. He picked up his mat and started walking around. The day on which this happened was a Sabbath.

When the Jewish leaders saw the man carrying his mat, they said to him, "This is the Sabbath! No one is allowed to carry a mat on the Sabbath."

But he replied, "The man who healed me told me to pick up my mat and walk."

They asked him, "Who is this man that told you to pick up your mat and walk?" But he did not know who Jesus was, and Jesus had left because of the crowd.

Later, Jesus met the man in the temple and told him, "You are now well. But don't sin any more or something worse might happen to you." The man left and told the leaders that Jesus was the one who had healed him. They started making a lot of trouble for Jesus because he did things like this on the Sabbath.

But Jesus said, "My Father has never stopped working, and that is why I keep on working." Now the leaders wanted to kill Jesus for two reasons. First, he had broken the law of the Sabbath. But even worse, he had said that God was his Father, which made him equal with God.

 Sign 4: Jesus cares for us in ways that matter

John 6:1–21

Jesus crossed Lake Galilee, which was also known as Lake Tiberias. A large crowd had seen him perform miracles to heal the sick, and those people went with him. It was almost time for the Jewish festival of Passover, and Jesus went up on a mountain with his disciples and sat down.

When Jesus saw the large crowd coming towards him, he asked Philip, "Where will we get enough food to feed all these people?" He said this to test Philip, since he already knew what he was going to do.

Philip answered, "Don't you know that it would take almost a year's wages just to buy only a little bread for each of these people?"

Andrew, the brother of Simon Peter, was one of the disciples. He spoke up and said, "There is a boy here who has five small loaves of barley bread and two fish. But what good is that with all these people?"

The ground was covered with grass, and Jesus told his disciples to make everyone sit down. About five thousand men were in the crowd. Jesus took the bread in his hands and gave thanks to God. Then he passed the bread to the people, and he did the same with the fish, until everyone had plenty to eat.

The people ate all they wanted, and Jesus told his disciples to gather up the leftovers, so that nothing would be wasted. The disciples gathered them up and filled twelve large baskets with what was left over from the five barley loaves.

After the people had seen Jesus perform this miracle, they began saying, "This must be the Prophet who is to come into the world!" Jesus realized that they would try to force him to be their king. So he went up on a mountain, where he could be alone.

That evening, Jesus' disciples went down to the lake. They got into a boat and set off for Capernaum. Later that evening Jesus had still not come to them, and a strong wind was making the water rough.

When the disciples had rowed for five or six kilometres, they saw Jesus walking on the water. He kept coming closer to the boat, and they were terrified. But he said, "I am Jesus! Don't be afraid!" The disciples wanted to take him into the boat, but suddenly the boat reached the shore where they were headed.

Photocopiable page

Sign 5: Jesus helps us understand God

John 9:1–11,18–28,34–38

As Jesus walked along, he saw a man who had been blind since birth. Jesus' disciples asked, "Teacher, why was this man born blind? Was it because he or his parents sinned?"

"No, it wasn't!" Jesus answered. "But because of his blindness, you will see God perform a miracle for him. As long as it is day, we must do what the one who sent me wants me to do. When night comes, no one can work. While I am in the world, I am the light for the world."

 After Jesus said this, he spat on the ground. He made some mud and smeared it on the man's eyes. Then he said, "Go and wash off the mud in Siloam Pool." The man went and washed in Siloam, which means "One who is sent". When he had washed off the mud, he could see.

The man's neighbours and the people who had seen him begging wondered if he really could be the same man. Some of them said he was the same beggar, while others said he only looked like him. But he told them, "I am that man."

 "Then how can you see?" they asked.

He answered, "Someone named Jesus made some mud and smeared it on my eyes. He told me to go and wash it off in Siloam Pool. When I did, I could see."

But the Jewish leaders would not believe that the man had once been blind. They sent for his parents and asked them, "Is this the son that you said was born blind? How can he now see?"

The man's parents answered, "We are certain that he is our son, and we know that he was born blind. But we don't know how he got his sight or who gave it to him. Ask him! He is old enough to speak for himself."

The man's parents said this because they were afraid of the Jewish leaders. The leaders had already agreed that no one was to have anything to do with anyone who said Jesus was the Messiah.

The leaders called the man back and said, "Swear by God to tell the truth! We know that Jesus is a sinner."

The man replied, "I don't know if he is a sinner or not. All I know is that I used to be blind, but now I can see!"

"What did he do to you?" the Jewish leaders asked. "How did he heal your eyes?"

The man answered, "I have already told you once, and you refused to listen. Why do you want me to tell you again? Do you also want to become his disciples?"

The leaders insulted the man and said, "You are his follower! …"

Then they said, "You can never come back into any of our meeting places!"

When Jesus heard what had happened, he went and found the man. Then Jesus asked, "Do you have faith in the Son of Man?"

He replied, "Sir, if you will tell me who he is, I will put my faith in him."

"You have already seen him," Jesus answered, "and right now he is talking with you."

The man said, "Lord, I put my faith in you!" Then he worshipped Jesus.

Photocopiable page

Sign 6: Jesus gives new life

John 11:1–8,17,20–36,38–44

A man called Lazarus was sick in the village of Bethany. He had two sisters, Mary and Martha … The sisters sent a message to the Lord and told him that his good friend Lazarus was sick.

When Jesus heard this, he said, "His sickness won't end in death. It will bring glory to God and his Son."

Jesus loved Martha and her sister and brother. But he stayed where he was for two more days. Then he said to his disciples, "Now we will go back to Judea."

"Teacher," they said, "the people there want to stone you to death! Why do you want to go back?"

When Jesus got to Bethany, he found that Lazarus had already been in the tomb four days.

When Martha heard that Jesus had arrived, she went out to meet him, but Mary stayed in the house. Martha said to Jesus, "Lord, if you had been here, my brother would not have died. Yet even now I know that God will do anything you ask."

Jesus told her, "Your brother will live again!"

Martha answered, "I know that he will be raised to life on the last day, when all the dead are raised."

Jesus then said, "I am the one who raises the dead to life! Everyone who has faith in me will live, even if they die. And everyone who lives because of faith in me will never really die. Do you believe this?"

"Yes, Lord!" she replied. "I believe that you are Christ, the Son of God. You are the one we hoped would come into the world."

After Martha said this, she went and privately said to her sister Mary, "The Teacher is here, and he wants to see you." As soon as Mary heard this, she got up and went out to Jesus. He was still outside the village where Martha had gone to meet him. Many people had come to comfort Mary, and when they saw her quickly leave the house, they thought she was going out to the tomb to cry. So they followed her.

Mary went to where Jesus was. Then as soon as she saw him, she knelt at his feet and said, "Lord, if you had been here, my brother would not have died."

When Jesus saw that Mary and the people with her were crying, he was terribly upset and asked, "Where have you put his body?"

They replied, "Lord, come and you will see."

Jesus started crying, and the people said, "See how much he loved Lazarus."

Jesus was still terribly upset. So he went to the tomb, which was a cave with a stone rolled against the entrance. Then he told the people to roll the stone away. But Martha said, "Lord, you know that Lazarus has been dead four days, and there will be a bad smell."

Jesus replied, "Didn't I tell you that if you had faith, you would see the glory of God?"

After the stone had been rolled aside, Jesus looked up towards heaven and prayed, "Father, I thank you for answering my prayer. I know that you always answer my prayers. But I said this, so that the people here would believe that you sent me."

When Jesus had finished praying, he shouted, "Lazarus, come out!" The man who had been dead came out. His hands and feet were wrapped with strips of burial cloth, and a cloth covered his face. Jesus then told the people, "Untie him and let him go."

 Final sign-up: What about us?

John 20:30–31

Jesus performed many other miracles for his disciples, and not all of them are written in this book. But these are written so that you will put your faith in Jesus as the Messiah and the Son of God. If you have faith in him, you will have true life.

⊕ Sign 7: Jesus is alive forever!

John 20:1–18

On Sunday morning while it was still dark, Mary Magdalene went to the tomb and saw that the stone had been rolled away from the entrance. She ran to Simon Peter and to Jesus' favourite disciple and said, "They have taken the Lord from the tomb! We don't know where they have put him."

Peter and the other disciple set off for the tomb. They ran side by side, until the other disciple ran faster than Peter and got there first. He bent over and saw the strips of linen cloth lying inside the tomb, but he did not go in.

When Simon Peter got there, he went into the tomb and saw the strips of cloth. He also saw the piece of cloth that had been used to cover Jesus' face. It was rolled up and in a place by itself. The disciple who got there first then went into the tomb, and when he saw it, he believed. At that time Peter and the other disciple did not know that the Scriptures said Jesus would rise to life. So the two of them went back to the other disciples.

Mary Magdalene stood crying outside the tomb. She was still weeping, when she stooped down and saw two angels inside. They were dressed in white and were sitting where Jesus' body had been. One was at the head and the other was at the foot. The angels asked Mary, "Why are you crying?" She answered, "They have taken away my Lord's body! I don't know where they have put him."

As soon as Mary said this, she turned around and saw Jesus standing there. But she did not know who he was. Jesus asked her, "Why are you crying? Who are you looking for?"

She thought he was the gardener and said, "Sir, if you have taken his body away, please tell me, so I can go and get him."

Then Jesus said to her, "Mary!"

She turned and said to him, "Rabboni." The Aramaic word "Rabboni" means "Teacher".

Jesus told her, "Don't hold on to me! I have not yet gone to the Father. But tell my disciples that I am going to the one who is my Father and my God, as well as your Father and your God." Mary Magdalene then went and told the disciples that she had seen the Lord. She also told them what he had said to her.

John 21:1–14

Jesus later appeared to his disciples along the shore of Lake Tiberias. Simon Peter, Thomas the Twin, Nathanael from Cana in Galilee, and the brothers James and John, were there, together with two other disciples. Simon Peter said, "I'm going fishing!"

The others said, "We will go with you." They went out in their boat. But they didn't catch a thing that night.

Early the next morning Jesus stood on the shore, but the disciples did not realize who he was. Jesus shouted, "Friends, have you caught anything?"

"No!" they answered.

So he told them, "Let your net down on the right side of your boat, and you will catch some fish."

They did, and the net was so full of fish that they could not drag it up into the boat.

Jesus' favourite disciple told Peter, "It's the Lord!" When Simon heard that it was the Lord, he put on the clothes that he had taken off while he was working. Then he jumped into the water. The boat was only about a hundred metres from shore. So the other disciples stayed in the boat and dragged in the net full of fish.

When the disciples got out of the boat, they saw some bread and a charcoal fire with fish on it. Jesus told his disciples, "Bring some of the fish you have just caught." Simon Peter got back into the boat and dragged the net to shore. In it were one hundred and fifty-three large fish, but still the net did not rip.

Jesus said, "Come and eat!" But none of the disciples dared ask who he was. They knew he was the Lord. Jesus took the bread in his hands and gave some of it to his disciples. He did the same with the fish. This was the third time that Jesus appeared to his disciples after he was raised from death.

Photocopiable page

Awesome!
God is an awesome God

God is an awesome God,
And he's full of amazing, wonderful love.
God is an awesome God,
And the name of his Son is Jesus.
God is an awesome God,
And he's full of amazing, wonderful love.
God is an awesome God,
And the name of his Son is Jesus.

Jesus did the impossible,
He turned water into wine;
He healed the sick and he raised the dead,
He gives new life, this is what he said:
'Follow me! And I will be with you.
Follow me! And I will be with you.
Follow me! And I will be with you.'

© Leanne Mitchell 2004, administered by Scripture Union

CCLI number _____

God is an awesome God

Leanne Mitchell

© Leanne Mitchell 2004, administered by Scripture Union

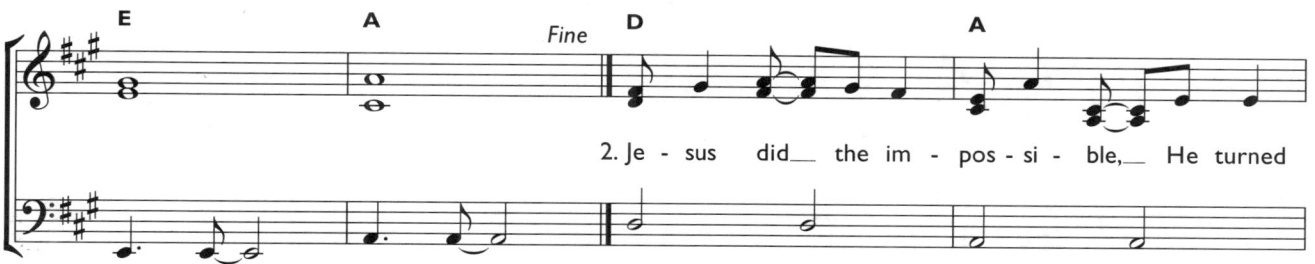
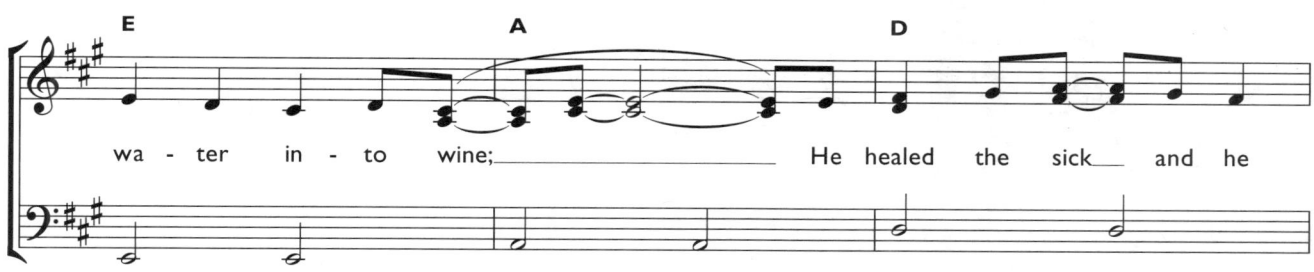

Awesome!

Staple 3

All about you!

Age: _____
Birthday: _____
I am a boy / girl

W I am _____ tall

H My eyes are _____

O My hair colour is _____

A Fave food: _____

M Fave team: _____

I Fave TV show: _____

Staple 4

Staple 2 _____ Staple 1
Name: _____
Address: _____

1
2
3
4
5
Emmaus
Jerusalem
Bethlehem
Bethany
Jericho
Nazareth
Cana
Capernaum
Miles
0
10
20

One o'clock

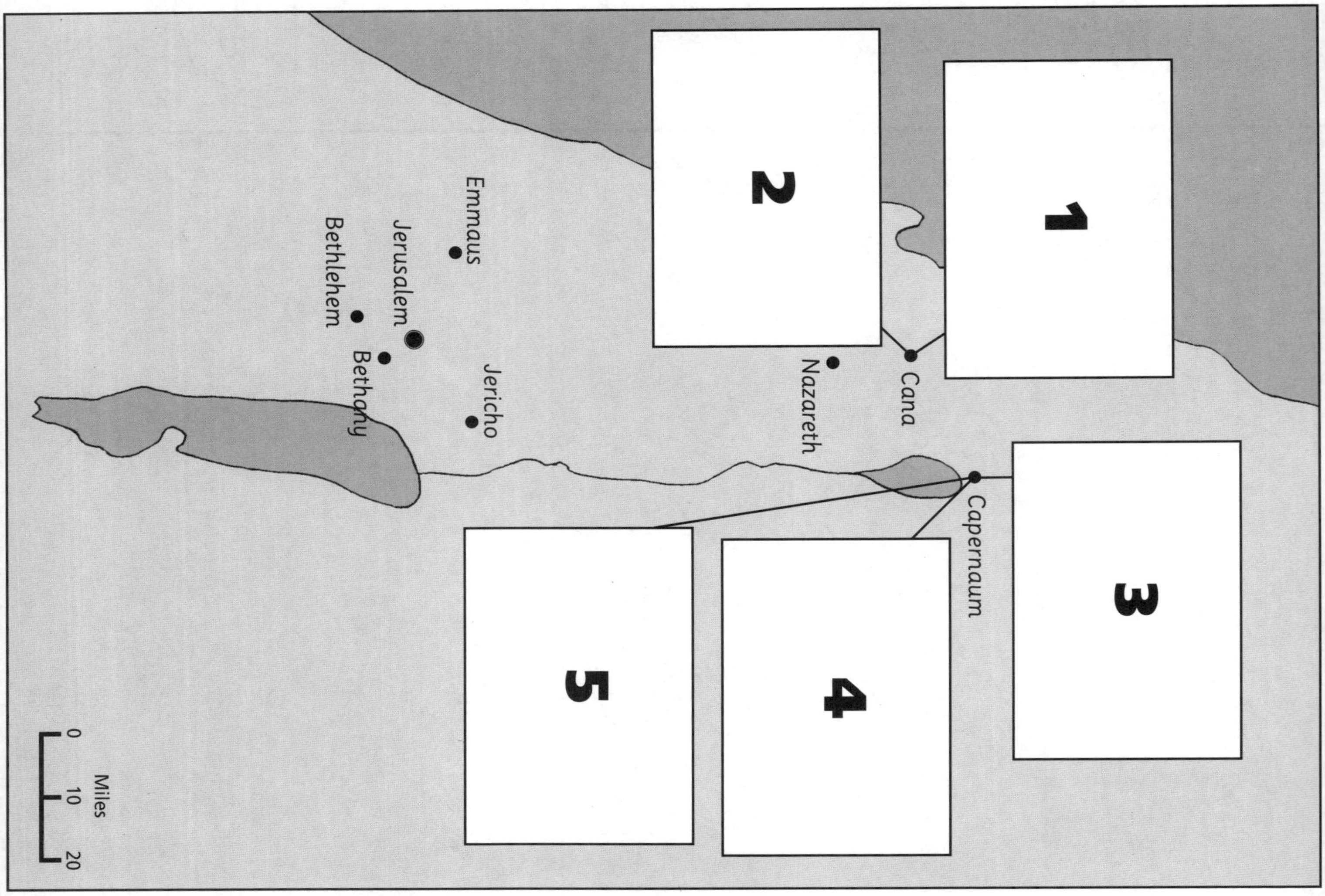

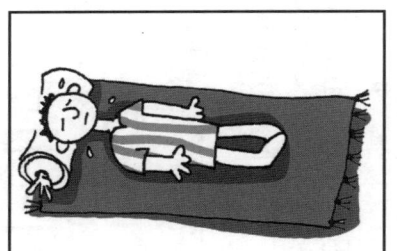

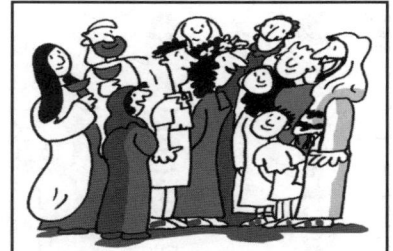

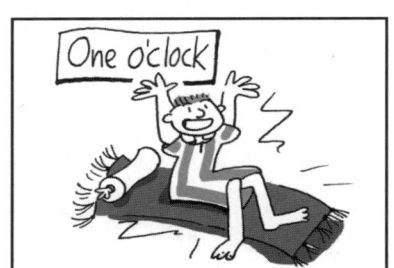

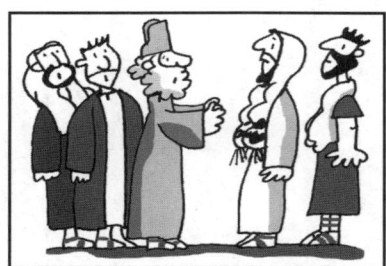

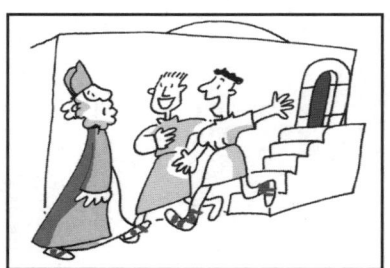

Photocopiable page 25

Jesus replied, "There are some things that people cannot do, but God can do anything!"

Luke 18:37

Photocopiable page

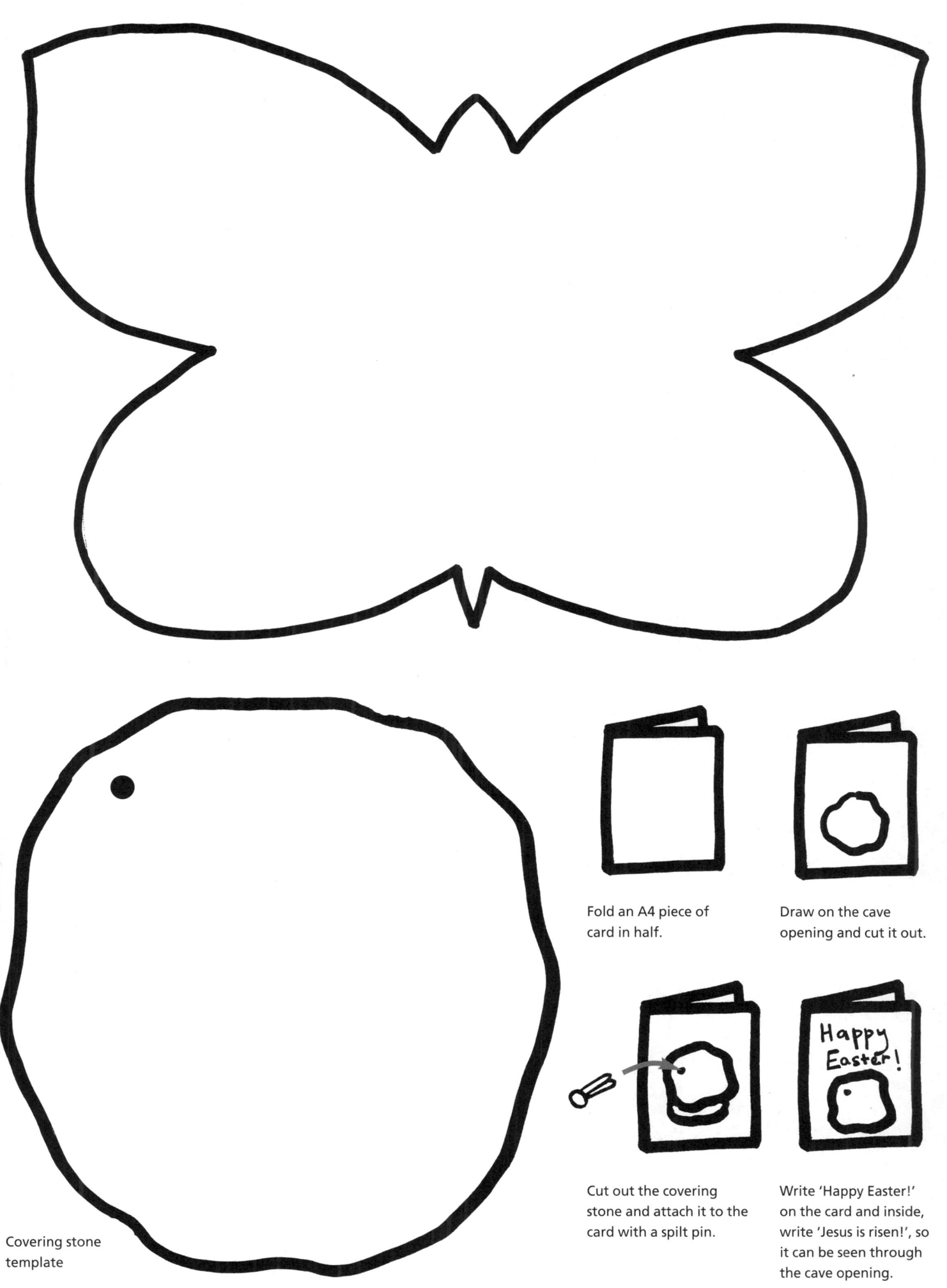

Fold an A4 piece of card in half.

Draw on the cave opening and cut it out.

Cut out the covering stone and attach it to the card with a spilt pin.

Write 'Happy Easter!' on the card and inside, write 'Jesus is risen!', so it can be seen through the cave opening.

Covering stone template

Photocopiable page

Jesus has God's power

Jesus turns water into wine

Eye openers

Welcome the children to Awesome! Introduce yourself and any other adult helpers.

Explain that at each Awesome! session, everyone will discover a sign that tells them something about Jesus. If you are not going to make either the Sparkling specs or the Flip-files, you may want to ensure each child has a badge so that you can remember names and create a sense of belonging. This is especially important if it is the first time you have run a club like this.

01 Sparkling specs
(10–20 minutes)

What you need
- Sparkling specs from page 22, photocopied onto card, for each child
- Scissors
- Hole punch
- Two split pins per child
- Selection of art materials, eg glitter, tinsel, glue, coloured pens, glitter paint, shiny paper

What you do
Each child cuts out the frame and arms of their spectacles and puts their name on the flash. Encourage the children to decorate the frames with whatever materials are available. Punch holes in the frame and arms where shown and fix them together with the split pin. Check that they fit the child. Encourage the children to wear the specs during Fact finders, but they may get in the way if worn for the whole session!

To extend the activity, make a specs case: fold a piece of card in half and stick down three sides to make a case that will hold the specs. You could keep hold of these so that the specs can be given out and worn at the start of each session.

If any of the leaders wear glasses, they could talk about how that is one way of describing someone. Talk about other ways or signs that show we are all different, signs that say something about us. For example, hair colour, height, food likes and dislikes. (Be aware that some children are bullied because they wear glasses so do not draw attention to any child who wears glasses unless you know they are happy about it.)

02 Flip-files
(10–20 minutes)

What you need
- A Flip-file for each child and adult copied from page 23 (use different coloured paper as a way of dividing the children into groups)
- A pen for each person
- Staplers
- A tape measure

What you do
Divide the children into small groups, each with an adult helper. Give everyone (adults included) a Flip-file template and a pen. Ask them to write their name and other details in the space on the right-hand side (help them if necessary). Then fold back along the dotted lines, so that the paper forms a sort of folder. Staple the paper where shown. The flap with 'Awesome!' written on should cover the name and address details, but leave the 'All about you' section visible (make sure you don't staple this flap down!). As the back of the Flip-file is blank, the children could draw a self-portrait in that space. You could take a photo of each child and stick it on their file, ready for the next session.

When everyone has had time to complete a Flip-file, select one at random. Read out the details from the 'All about you' section. Can anyone guess whose Flip-file it is? Lift the flap to reveal the name!

Explain that as everyone gets to know each other better, they will be able to guess more easily. Invite each small group to muddle up the Flip-files they have and see if they can identify each owner in turn by reading the signs but not opening the flap.

Sign 1

John 2:1–11

Aim To help children enter the atmosphere of a wedding where Jesus did an extraordinary thing in an everyday situation. Jesus' power is still available for us in everyday situations when things go wrong.

Notes for you
In the first century, wedding celebrations lasted for several days. Food, and especially wine, were an important part of the festivities. It was an embarrassing social disgrace if the supply of wine ran dry. Jesus showed his concern at this and announced his arrival on the scene with his first miracle – a demonstration of his God-given power over the created world. As you introduce this *Awesome!* programme, pray that the children will discover not only that Jesus is alive today but also that his power is still very much at work.

In this first session, completing the Sparkling specs or the Flip-files will take at least ten minutes, so allow extra time for *Eye Openers*.

AWESOME!

1

Checklist
- A photocopy of the Flip-file template on page 23 or the Sparkling specs on page 22 for each person
- A copy of John's Gospel for each child, or a photocopy of the Bible verses on page 14 for each child (optional)
- Materials for your choice of activities for *Eye openers*, *Fact finders* and *Sign spotters*

When you see this logo, the activity is particularly appropriate for smaller groups.

When you see this logo, the activity will work well with older children.

O3 Where are we?
(3 minutes)

What you need
- Props for a wedding: a hat, flowers, an invitation, a bride's veil, confetti (include less obvious objects such as a ribbon, a handkerchief, car keys, a rolling pin)

What you do
Explain that the children need to guess from the clues they are given where they think they are for this session. For example, they could be in the desert or at school… Show the children the wedding items one at a time, starting with the least obvious. Invite them to suggest where they think they might be, but keep them guessing and don't reveal the correct answer until you have shown them all the items. This time they are at a wedding!

O4 Water game
(5–10 minutes)

If you are going to do *Sign spotters* 'Fill the jars' you will not want to play this now.

What you need
- Teams of 6–10 children (smaller groups could play this against the clock)
- A bucket of water and an empty bucket per team
- Small container per team (eg yogurt pot)
- Stopwatch
- Clean-up facilities

What you do
Line up the teams behind their full bucket and place the empty bucket at the other end of your playing area. On the signal to start, the first person in each team fills up their container with water, runs to the other bucket and empties the water into it. Once they have returned, the second person in the team goes. At the end of a given time, measure to see which team has poured the most into their bucket.

Discuss how heavy the buckets are as a way of preparing for the weight of water in the jars in the story.

Alternative 'dry' games could be team games that involve moving bulky objects such as a fat cushion from one end of the room to the other. Or try a tug of war.

> *The girls just loved this game and pleaded for us to play it next week!*
> Chris, Croxley Green

O5 Awesome! snack bar
(5–15 minutes)

What you need
- A table set up as a snack bar
- A large piece of white paper painted with red stripes to make an awning
- Snack-bar refreshments for the children – remember to check for any food allergies

What you do
Set up a counter-style snack bar with a table and an awning. Serve drinks and different bagged snacks such as crisps, cheese puffs, nachos or chocolate biscuits (often available in special offer multi-packs from supermarkets). Remember that supportive church members are often happy to help with catering, so make good use of them – home-baked cakes are always popular!

To make it a bit different, you may like to operate a simple token system each session, so that the children exchange tokens for a drink and a packet of crisps, for example. If necessary, extra tokens could be an incentive for good behaviour, but make sure that everyone gets an extra token for something at least once.

Choose two or three children to stand behind the counter and serve the others. Make a note of which children serve each time so that everyone has a turn. Encourage the adult helpers to chat with the children while you have your refreshments.

Fact finders

①1 The wedding
(5 minutes)

What you do
Explain that Jesus went to a wedding with his friends and it was there that he did his first miracle – something amazing that couldn't be explained. It was a sign. Show the video clip *The wedding*.

①2 Read all about it!
(3 minutes)

What you need
- A copy of John's Gospel for each child, a photocopy of the Bible verses on page 14 for each child (optional) or an acetate version, plus overhead projector
- A whiteboard or flip chart paper and pen

What you do

Tell the children that the true story they have just watched is from the book of John in the Bible. John was one of Jesus' special friends and he spent a lot of time with Jesus. John wrote down the awesome things that Jesus did and said, so that people all over the world could hear about Jesus. This is what he wrote.

Read John 2:1–11 and encourage the children to listen out for the numbers in the story. Whenever a number is read out, ask the children to put their hand up and write it on the board. (The 'no more wine' could be a zero.)

3 What really happened?
(5 minutes)

What you do
Read the alternative version of this session's story (below) to everyone. Ask each child to listen carefully and put their hand up if they spot a mistake. They have to tell you what the correct version is. Alternatively, as you read the story, the children could follow it in their John's Gospel or the photocopy of the Bible verses from page 14. You could award points or snack-bar tokens for each answer.

John 2:1–11
Mary, the aunt *(mother)* of Jesus, was at a birthday party *(wedding feast)* in the village of Capernaum *(Cana)* in Galilee. Jesus and some children *(his disciples)* had also been invited, but couldn't go *(and were there)*.

When the orange juice *(wine)* was all gone, Martha *(Mary)* said to Jesus, 'They don't have any more lemonade *(wine)*.'

Jesus replied, 'Mother, my time hasn't yet come! You must always tell me what to do *(must not tell me what to do)*.'

Mary then said to the bride and bridegroom *(servants)*, 'Do whatever you think is best *(whatever Jesus tells you to do)*.'

At the feast there were three *(six)* stone water jars that were used by the people for drinking *(washing)* in the way that their religion said they must. Each jar held about a litre *(100 litres)*. Jesus told the servants to fill them half full *(to the top)* with water. Then after the jars had been half-filled *(filled)*, he said, 'Now take some water and give it to all the guests *(the man in charge of the feast)*.'

The servants didn't listen to Jesus *(did as Jesus told them)*, and the man in charge looked at *(drank)* some of the water that had now turned into coffee *(wine)*. He knew *(did not know)* where the wine had come from, but the servants didn't *(did)*. He called the bride's mother *(bridegroom)* over and said, 'The best wine is always served last *(first)*. Then after the servants *(guests)* have had a little *(plenty)*, the other wine is served. But you have kept the best until last!' This was Jesus' second *(first)* miracle.

Sign spotters

Choose from the following activities:

1 Fill the jars
(10–15 minutes)

What you need
- A jug or storage container to represent a water jar for each team
- A plastic cup for each team
- A large bucket of water to represent the well
- A litre bottle
- A measuring jug
- Plastic covering for the floor, if playing indoors
- Clean-up facilities

What you do
Show the children the litre bottle and ask how many litres of water the servants had to collect from the well – the answer is 600, because each of the six jars held 100 litres. In those days there were no taps, so the servants would have had to make hundreds of trips to the well!

Give each person a plastic cup. Invite each team to stand in a line one behind the other around the bucket of water (the well), so that the lines form a star with the bucket at the centre. Place a water jar at each end of the line.

On the signal to start, the first person in each team fills their cup from the well, then tips the water into the next person's cup and so on down the line. The last person empties it into the 'jar'. How much can each team 'carry' in five minutes?

Give the groups a time limit and then have a measuring ceremony to see which group has managed to fill their jar with the most water.

Explain that what Jesus did next wasn't magic, it was something very special that only he could do, because he had God's power. The Bible calls it a miracle. Awesome!

We had a refreshment break at this point. The lemonade drinks came from a 2-litre lemonade bottle and then we worked out how many drinks they would have got from 600 litres of wine, using the whiteboard. It worked well!

Rosey, Sutton

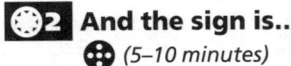 And the sign is...
(5–10 minutes)

What you need
- A large sheet of paper and a thick felt-tip pen
- A jug of water, a glass and an egg cup

What you do
In the style of the game Hangman, draw a dash on the paper for each of the letters of the following Bible verse, leaving a space between the words:
The Father loves his Son and has put everything in his power. John 3:35
Explain that when the blank Bible verse is completed it will explain how Jesus turned water into wine.

Use the Good News Bible, as other versions do not include the word 'power'.

Invite everyone in turn to give you a letter of the alphabet. Write it on the correct dash. Each time a letter suggested is not in any of the words, choose a child to pour an egg cup full water into the glass. It is a race to see if the verse can be completed before the glass is full! When you have completed all the words, say the verse together several times, then remove the sheet of paper and ask if anyone can remember it. Ask the following questions:
- Who is the Father? God
- Who is his Son? Jesus
- What has God put in Jesus' power? Everything

Ask the children to complete these sentences:
Jesus is God's … Son
Jesus has God's … Power
God's power is … Awesome!
The first sign is:
Jesus has God's power. Awesome!

 Going to a wedding
(10–20 minutes)

What you need
- Newspapers
- Crêpe paper and tissue paper (optional)
- Scissors and staplers
- Sticky tape and string

What you do
Challenge everyone to make suitable wedding gear from the materials provided. Either: split the children into smaller groups and ask them to make an outfit (hat, bow tie etc) for one of their group. Or: ask the children to make something that they themselves might wear to a wedding. Allow at least ten minutes for this and then have a parade of the results.

❝ *This was excellent as every child made something (flowers, a bow tie or a hat) and we enjoyed the parade afterwards.* ❞
Rosey, Sutton

Take this opportunity, as all the children work on their wedding clothes, to talk about how Jesus was able to do such an extraordinary thing. You might like to ask questions like these:
- How would you feel if you were at a wedding and there was no food or drink left?
- What do you think Jesus' mum, Mary, was expecting Jesus to do when she told him there was no wine left? Go out to find some more? Get cross with the man who was in charge of the banquet?
- How would you have felt when you discovered that the water had been turned into wine and it was really, really good wine too?
- Why do you think Jesus was able to do something like that? (If you have done 'And the sign is…', see if the children have understood the verse.)
- Can you think of any times when things have gone wrong and you can't think what you can do to make things better?
- (If appropriate) Do you think Jesus could do anything for you in times like that?

 What's awesome?
(5 minutes)

What you need
- The children's Flip-files/Sparkling specs cases
- Felt-tip pens or pencils
- Pieces of paper small enough to fit inside the Flip-files/Sparkling specs cases

What you do
At the end of the session, encourage the children to think about what they remember most about today's programme and write or draw it on a piece of paper. Chat with the children as they work, and help as necessary. When they have finished, keep their pieces of paper safe in the child's Flip-file/Sparkling specs case. Use this time to assess what the children have enjoyed and remembered. Is there anything you might want to do differently in the next session?

Awesome! prayers

Use one or both of these prayer ideas somewhere in your session.

Disaster prayers
(3 minutes)

What you need
- A cymbal, gong or something noisy to drop
- Whiteboard and marker pen

What you do
Invite the children to think of disasters that happen to them, such as breaking a leg, losing something important, the death of a pet. Draw a symbol of the disaster on the board and then bang the cymbal as a sign of the disaster. Be sensitive about what is shared. The death of a grandparent is a lasting 'disaster', whereas losing a mobile is bad news but not earth-shattering.

Then pray this prayer:

Jesus, thank you that you understand how we feel when things go badly wrong. Thank you that you have the power to put things right or make us feel OK about what's gone wrong. (Allow each child to picture one disaster in their minds.)
Please make a difference in the situations we have just thought of. Amen.

The Awesome! song
(5–10 minutes)

You will need
- The words to 'God is an awesome God' (see page 19)
- DVD player and the *Awesome!* DVD, or CD player and the CD *Light for Everyone*, or sheet music (see pages 20, 21) and piano/guitar

What you do
Teach the children this song and use it as your conversation with God today.

 Re-run
(5 minutes)

What you do
Just before the children leave you could show the video *The wedding* again. Parents who arrive early to collect their children will also see it!

Don't forget!
If you plan to make use of the Flip-files or Sparkling specs in future weeks, remember to collect them from the children before they leave. Keep them in alphabetical order, ready to distribute at the beginning of the next session.

AWESOME!

Sign 2
John 4:46–54

Aim To realise that Jesus has the power to heal someone just by saying the word, which seems impossible! Talk about how Jesus can heal people whom the children know and how we can ask him to do this.

Notes for you
The fact that Jesus healed the sick boy was a miracle in itself. However, he also healed him immediately, and from a distance! This was further proof that he was the Son of God and, as a result, the man and everyone in his family put their trust in Jesus.
Pray that the children will enjoy this *Awesome!* session and keep coming each time, so that they can discover more about Jesus' love for them.

Jesus can do the impossible

Jesus heals an official's son

Eye openers
Welcome the children to Awesome! If there are any newcomers, introduce yourself and any other adult helpers and make sure they complete a Flip-file or put on their badge or Sparkling specs. Give out any notices and mention any children who have had birthdays since you last met. If some children arrive early, they could colour in the pictures that accompany the map for 'Read all about it'. Alternatively, you could start making the Awesome! banner described on page 13.

O1 Flip-files
(3–5 minutes)

What you need
- Each person's Flip-file

What you do
Divide the children into small groups, each with an adult helper. The groups should muddle up the Flip-files and the group members should take it in turns to read out someone's favourite food, as written in the file. The others in the group should try and guess who that person is.

O2 Possible or impossible?
(3–5 minutes)

What you do
Set the children some tasks that may be difficult but are possible, such as rubbing their tummy and patting their head at the same time, touching the floor with the palms of their hands without bending their knees, wiggling their ears and raising one eyebrow. Give them a chance to demonstrate 'party tricks' – this could be an opportunity to involve any quieter children. Then challenge them to see if they can do the impossible. Can anyone use their tongue to touch their forehead? Can anyone fold a piece of paper in half more than eight times? Can anyone fly? It's impossible to do some things.

> *The children were keen to show us their crossed eyes and rolling tongues.*
> Jean, Aldridge

> *The children demonstrated their rippling stomachs. We had to keep it quick or it would have got out of control.*
> Rosey, Sutton

O3 Team games
(As long as you wish)

What you need
- Hats, gloves and scarves or obstacles

What you do
If you are going to use hats for the drama or interview, play a mad clothes race. Divide the children into teams and give each team a hat, a scarf and a pair of gloves. Each team member has to put all three on before they can run to a target and back. Then they take off the hat, gloves and scarf and give them to the next child. Alternatively, devise an obstacle course that is really challenging, depending upon the ability of the children. Some of the tasks should be almost impossible – that is the theme of today!

O4 Quiz impossible
(5 minutes)

What you need
- Quiz questions
- Paper for writing down the word 'impossible'

What you do
Devise a quiz with ten non-Biblical questions, where the initial letters of the answers spell the word 'impossible', for example:
What is the name for an eskimo's home? (*Igloo*)
What football team plays in a red strip and plays at Old Trafford? (*Manchester United*)

JESUS CAN DO THE IMPOSSIBLE

What is a small version of a flute called? *(Piccolo)*

Make the questions suitable for your age group and as contemporary as possible.

Explain that you are going to look at a story about something quite impossible!

⚫5 Awesome! snack bar
(5–15 minutes)

What you need
- A table and awning set up as a snack bar (see Session 1)
- Snack-bar refreshments for the children – remember to check for any food allergies

What you do
Serve the children with food and drinks. Encourage the adult helpers to chat with the children while you have your refreshments.

Fact finders

⚫1 The prince's son
(5 minutes)

What you do
Explain that in this true story from the Bible, Jesus did two things that were impossible. They were another sign, telling us more about Jesus. Show the video clip *The prince's son*. Note, the DVD episode calls the official a 'prince'. You may need to point that out to the children.

⚫2 Read all about it!
(5 minutes)

What you need
- A copy of John's Gospel for each child, or a photocopy of the Bible verses on page 14 for each child (optional)
- A photocopy of the map on page 24 – one per child or an enlarged copy for the whole group
- Scissors, glue and, if time, felt-tip pens

What you do
Give each person a map and a copy of the Bible verses and ask them to cut out the five pictures from the map. As they listen to the Bible verses or read them for themselves, they should put the pictures into the right place. Talk about just how far the official/prince had to walk to find Jesus. With a large group, enlarge the map with the five pictures using a photocopier. Give the pictures out to five groups of children and ask

them to stick their picture on the big map as the story is told.

> *The best bit was the amazement on the children's faces when they realised Jesus healed from a distance and at the exact time.*
> Cheryl, Cardiff

⚫3 The Awesome! song
(5–10 minutes)

What you need
- The words to 'God is an awesome God' (see page 19)
- DVD player and the *Awesome!* DVD, or CD player and the CD *Light for Everyone*, or sheet music (see pages 20,21) and piano/guitar

What you do
Sing the song! You may need to teach it again to any children who are new, or who have forgotten it since your last session!

Sign spotters

Choose from the following activities:

⚫1 What really happened?
(5 minutes)

What you need
- A microphone
- A leader to act as an interviewer

What you do
The interviewer moves around the group with the microphone and interviews different children in the style of an on-the-spot news reporter. The interviewer begins by saying, 'I'm here to investigate recent events surrounding the prince's son. What happened? Does anyone know?'

> *It helps if the interviewer has learnt the questions to make everything more spontaneous and genuine.*
> Rosey, Sutton

In case the children don't enter into the role play spontaneously, prime one or two adult helpers to be ready to answer – this will probably set the ball rolling. Then ask questions along the following lines:

Checklist
- The children's Flip-files or Sparkling specs for them to use, plus spares for newcomers
- A copy of John's Gospel for each child, or a photocopy of the Bible verses on page 14 for each child (optional)
- Materials for your choice of activities for *Eye openers*, *Fact finders* and *Sign spotters*
- Materials for the *Awesome!* banner (see page 13)

⚫ *When you see this logo, the activity is particularly appropriate for smaller groups.*

😊 *When you see this logo, the activity will work well with older children.*

- What was wrong with the prince's son?
- What did the prince say to Jesus?
- What did Jesus say would happen to his son?
- What did the prince do next?
- Do you think he believed Jesus?
- What happened when the prince was on the way home?
- What did the servants tell the prince?
- What did the prince and his family do?
- What does this tell us about Jesus?

2 And the sign is…
(5–10 minutes)

What you need
- Four different coloured copies of the jigsaw template on page 26

What you do
Before the session, cut up the four copies of the jigsaw and hide the pieces around the room. Explain to the children that they need to find a complete set of hidden jigsaw pieces, all the same colour. Once they have done this, can they work out what the memory verse is?

> ***Jesus replied, 'There are some things that people cannot do, but God can do anything!' Luke 18:27***

When they have done this, read the verse again, pausing before the words 'cannot do' and 'can do' to let the children say the appropriate word. Do this several times and then see if anyone can say the whole verse from memory. What about the verse they learned last session?

Help everyone to say John 3:35 together. Can they remember what the first sign was?

The second sign is:
Jesus can do the impossible. Awesome!

3 Play it again
 (15–30 minutes)

What you need
- Hats, or other accessories

What you do
Split the children into smaller groups, each group with an adult leader. Ask the groups to come up with a brief drama of today's story. Let them choose suitable hats or accessories for each of the characters. There could be three scenes as follows:

Scene 1: The prince is at home and his son is very ill. What does the prince decide to do?
Scene 2: The prince finds Jesus and asks him to help.
Scene 3: What happens when the prince meets the servants on his way home?

Keep it short and simple. Invite each group in turn to present their drama to everyone.

 The children love to choose a hat to suit their role – at least, they thought the hat suited the role!
Jean, Aldridge

4 Film show
(10–20 minutes)

Do this if you have children who enjoy craft or colouring. This is an opportunity for you to talk together as you make things. You could do this all together.

What you need
- The five pictures from the map, enlarged (see page 24)
- Card
- Cereal boxes (optional)
- Scissors, glue and felt-tip pens

What you do
Together, cut out the pictures and colour them in. Stick them to pieces of card. Cut out a television screen from one long side of a cereal box, making slits at the edge. Stick the five pictures together to make a continuous roll of film, which should slide through the box.

As you do this, chat with the children about the story using the following questions:
- How do people give orders to someone if they can't actually be heard?
- What do you think the prince was thinking about as he was travelling to Cana?
- Do you think he was disappointed that Jesus didn't go back to his home?
- If you had been the prince, how would you have felt as you walked back home again?
- What do you think the prince thought of Jesus after his son was healed?
- If Jesus did something like that to someone you loved, what would you think?

Be prepared to talk about a way in which Jesus has done something extraordinary like that in your life or for someone you know.

5 What's awesome?
(5 minutes)

What you need
- The children's Flip-files/Sparkling specs cases
- Felt-tip pens or pencils
- Pieces of paper small enough to fit inside the Flip-files/Sparkling specs cases

What you do
At the end of the session, encourage the children to think about what they remember most about today's programme and write or draw it on a piece of paper. Chat with the children as they work, and help as necessary. When they have finished, keep their pieces of paper safe in the child's Flip-file/Sparkling Specs case. What the children write may help you in planning the next session.

Don't forget!
Remember to collect the Flip-files and Sparkling specs from the children before they leave. The children could use the cases to store their maps, or their copy of this session's Bible verses. Keep the Flip-files and Sparkling specs in alphabetical order, ready to distribute at the beginning of the next session.

The idea for *Eye openers* 'Quiz impossible' came from *Ready! Steady! Assembly!* – a KS2 assembly book packed full of ideas for use in primary schools (SU, £6.00, 1 85999 189 0)

Awesome! prayers

Use one or both of these prayer ideas somewhere in your session.
(5 minutes)

Prayer for sick people

What you do
If you have not done *Sign spotters* 'Film show', talk about how God has healed someone that you know in a remarkable way. Then break into small groups, each with an adult helper, and encourage the children to mention anyone they know who is in need whom they could pray for. Invite the small groups to pray together – either silently or aloud. Close with the following prayer:

Thank you, God, for the awesome way in which Jesus healed the sick boy. Thank you that you can do anything. Please answer our prayers and help us to trust you, because you know what is best for each of the people we have prayed for. Amen.

Sticking plaster prayer

What you need
- Pens
- Plasters (some children are allergic to ordinary plasters, so use hypo-allergenic plasters)

What you do
Talk about how God heals, using your own experience. Give each child a sticking plaster and ask them to write on it the name of someone they know who is ill. They can stick the plaster to their hand. Ask Jesus to help each person to get better and allow a few seconds for the children to talk to God about the person on their plaster.

Sign 3

John 5:1–18

Aim To explore how Jesus knew all about what the man at the pool needed, unlike the powerful, rule-enforcing Pharisees. From this, we can come to know that Jesus knows exactly what we need and knows what is best for us.

Notes for you

This miracle shows how, on the Sabbath, Jesus made a sick man's need a priority, rather than strict observance of the rules. You will need to explain that God made the world in six days, then rested. So, God said that people should rest every seventh day. Over time, rules had grown up to enforce this, most of which seem absurd. Keeping these rules had become more important than knowing God, who had planned for us to rest. All this was a sign of Jesus' authority, sovereignty and compassion, in contrast to the Pharisees, who were concerned with upholding their traditions. They had little sympathy for the man who had been lying by the pool for 38 years! Jesus annoyed the Pharisees further by stating that God was his Father. Pray for each child, that they would realise that Jesus knows them and what is best for them.
Remember that some children will know a person who finds it hard to walk – you may have a child in your group who is wheelchair-bound. Be sensitive to their situation and what they can contribute.

Jesus knows what's best for us

Jesus heals the man by the pool

Eye openers

Welcome the children to Awesome! If there are any newcomers, introduce yourself and any other adult helpers and make sure someone helps them complete a Flip-file or put on their Sparkling specs. Make sure anyone who has had a birthday is made to feel special. You could start making, or carry on making, the Awesome! banner described on page 13 as children arrive.

O1 Jointed people
(15–20 minutes)

What you need
- Split-pin man copied from page 25, enough for one per child
- Split pins
- Scissors, felt-tip pens
- Glue and material for clothing

What you do
Encourage the children to cut out the man and colour him in. Alternatively, stick material on the man to make tatty clothing. Join the limbs together as shown on page 25. As you do this, talk about what it would feel like to be unable to walk or move your limbs. How do the children think other people would look at them? Help them see that to be unable to walk means that you are dependent on others and have specific needs.

Talk briefly with everyone about the last two sessions. Find out if anyone can remember the first two signs about Jesus – that he has God's power and he can do the impossible. What awesome things did Jesus do to show everyone this?

This took quite a long time but was a useful opportunity to build relationships as we talked together.
Rosey, Sutton

If you have a large group, you could make a large version of this and use it to talk about what you can and cannot do if you can't walk and how other people see you.

O2 Races without legs
(5 minutes)

What you need
- Equipment for races

What you do
Split the group into teams and have races that emphasise the need to use legs. For example, a three-legged race, wheelbarrow race, hopping race, shuffle on your bottom race (make sure your floor has no splinters!)

Take time to talk about the implications of not being able to walk and how people treat those who cannot walk.

O3 Imaginary jacuzzi!
(3 minutes)

What you do
Invite the group to find a space on the floor, make sure everyone is comfortable and get them to close their eyes. Imagine it is a hot, sunny day and they are beside a bubbling outdoor jacuzzi. Perhaps they can hear the birds singing and feel a gentle breeze. After a while, they might like a dip in the pool, so all they have to do is get up and jump in…

But what if they can't do that? Suppose they are paralysed, or so ill that they can't move at all? The water looks so nice, but they can't reach it. How does that make them feel? Encourage one or two children to share their feelings with everyone.

⊙4 Awesome! snack bar
(5–10 minutes)

What you need
- A table and awning set up as a snack bar (see Session 1)
- Snack-bar refreshments for the children – remember to check for any food allergies

What you do
Serve the children with food and drinks. Encourage the adult helpers to chat with the children while you have your refreshments.

> We developed the bubble theme and served Aero chocolate and sherbet flying saucers.
> *Jean, Aldridge*

Fact finders

◑1 The man at the pool
(5 minutes)

What you do
This is another sign that tells us more about Jesus. Show the video clip *The man at the pool*.

◑2 Read all about it!
(5 minutes)

What you need
- A copy of John's Gospel for each child, or a photocopy of the Bible verses on page 15 for each child (optional)
- A split-pin man for each child

What you do
Encourage everyone to sit or lie down. Give each person a copy of the Bible verses, which they can follow if they wish. Read out John 5:1–15 and, as you do so, ask the children to move their split-pin man to reflect the movements of the man. If you have just one large jointed man, the children can take it in turns to move him as the story unfolds.

◑3 What really happened?
(10 minutes)

What you need
- A sheet of paper numbered 1 to 10 for each small group
- Eight letter Ts and eight letter Fs for each group
- Glue sticks
- A prize for each group

What you do
Split the children into small groups. Give each group a sheet of paper numbered 1 to 10, eight Ts and Fs and a glue stick. Read John 5:1–18 to everyone.

Ask the children the questions below. Each group decides together whether the answer is true (T) or false (F), and sticks the right letter next to the number. When you have asked all the questions, give the answers and add up the scores. Explain that Jesus knew exactly what the man needed and what was best for him. What Jesus said to him was true, even though the Jewish leaders thought that what Jesus said was false.

■ TRUE OR FALSE?
1 This story happened at the pool of Bethzatha in Jerusalem. *(True.)*
2 Sick people were lying in the porches because they believed that the first into the bubbling water would be healed. *(True.)*
3 There was a man lying there who had been ill for 38 years. *(True.)*
4 The man called out loudly and asked Jesus to help him. *(False. Jesus asked him if he wanted to be healed.)*
5 Jesus told the man to pick up his mat and walk. *(True.)*
6 The man trusted Jesus and so he was able to get up and walk. *(True.)*
7 The Jewish leaders told the man that he shouldn't be walking around on the Sabbath. *(False. They told the man that he shouldn't be carrying his mat on the Sabbath.)*
8 The man didn't know who it was who had healed him, when it happened. *(True.)*
9 Jesus met the man again in the market. *(False. He met him in the temple.)*
10 The leaders were angry when Jesus said that God was his Father. *(True.)*

Checklist
- The children's Flip-files or Sparkling specs for them to use, plus spares for newcomers
- A copy of John's Gospel for each child, or a photocopy of the Bible verses on page 15 for each child (optional)
- Materials for your choice of activities for *Eye openers*, *Fact finders* and *Sign spotters*
- Materials for the *Awesome!* banner (see page 13)

When you see this logo, the activity is particularly appropriate for smaller groups.

When you see this logo, the activity will work well with older children.

3

Sign spotters

Choose from the following activities:

1 Bubble printing
(5 minutes)

You could combine this with the prayer activity. Half the children could do this while the other half do the prayer writing.

What you need
- Washing-up liquid
- Plastic cups
- Ready-mix blue or green paint and water
- Straws
- White A4 paper

What you do
Squeeze some washing-up liquid into a plastic cup, along with some ready-mix paint and a small amount of water. Blow through a straw into the mixture until there is a good froth of bubbles coming over the top of the cup. Gently place a piece of paper on top of the bubbles. Remove the paper, blow again and place a different part of the paper on the bubbles. Repeat until the paper is covered with bubble prints.

Everyone got really involved in the prayer writing and the bubble printing.
Jean, Aldridge

2 And the sign is…
(5–15 minutes)

What you need
- A Christian volunteer who is willing to talk about a time when they had a particular need and realised that Jesus not only knew all about it, but knew what was best for them. See page 8 for ideas on sharing our faith and experiences with children.

What you do
Introduce the visitor to the children and let them share their experiences. If appropriate, allow time for the children to ask questions. Then let them explore how Jesus singled the lame man out, healed him and found him again in the temple. You might want to adapt the following questions:
- What would it be like not to be able to walk?
- How do you think the man could cope with waiting year after year in the hope that the water might bubble and he might be the first into it?
- How does Jesus show that he cared for this man?
- What in particular do we want people to know about us? (This could provoke personal observations or more objective ones.)
- What would it mean to us to know that Jesus knows what's best for us?

The third sign is:
Jesus knows what's best for us. Awesome!

3 Action replay!
(15–30 minutes)

What you need
- A camera (digital, Polaroid or one with film)

What you do
Tell the group that you are going to create a photo story about Jesus and the man at the pool. Together, create scenes to represent the stages of the story and take a picture of each one. You could take several shots of each scene or get double prints developed so that the photos could be shared among the children.

We used a Polaroid camera with instant photos. This worked really well!
Jean, Aldridge

4 What's awesome?
(5 minutes)

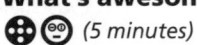

What you need
- The children's Flip-files/Sparkling specs cases
- Felt-tip pens or pencils
- Pieces of paper small enough to fit inside the Flip-files/Sparkling specs cases

What you do
At the end of the session, encourage the children to think about what they remember most about today's programme and write or draw it on a piece of paper. Chat with the children as they work, and help as necessary. When they have finished, keep their pieces of paper safe in the child's Flip-file/Sparkling specs case. Use this time to assess what the children have enjoyed and remembered. Is there anything you might want to do differently in the next session?

5 The Awesome! song
(5–10 minutes)

You will need
- The words to 'God is an awesome God' (see page 19)
- DVD player and the *Awesome!* DVD, or CD player and the CD *Light for Everyone*, or sheet music (see pages 20, 21) and piano/guitar

What you do
Finish your session by singing the *Awesome!* song. You may need to teach it again to any children who are new, or who have forgotten it since your last session!

Don't forget!
If you did 'Action replay!' remember to get the film processed, if that's the kind of camera you used.

Awesome! prayers

Use one or both of these prayer ideas somewhere in your session.
(5 minutes)

Bubble prayers

What you need
- Some bubble prints made before the session, and cut into interesting shapes
- Pens and pencils

What you do
If you have a large group, you may need to do this in two parts.

Ask the children to think about anyone they know (including themselves) who might have a particular need. The children can write or draw this person on the bubble print and ask God to be with them in a special way. Reassure everyone that handwriting and spelling don't matter at all!

The children could take these home or you could stick these on a poster, unless the prayers are very personal.

Bubble praise

What you need
- Three tubs of bubble mixture
- A large sheet of paper

What you do
Explain that they are going to create some prayers of praise and thanks to God, for Jesus had shown his power to heal and his love for this man. Ask the children to share anything for which they want to thank God. Write their comments down on the sheet of paper.

Ask three children to come to the front to blow bubbles after each phrase of thanks as the children say, 'God you are awesome!'
For example:
Dear God, we thank you that Gemma's mum is better now.
Altogether: God you are awesome!
(Blow bubbles.)
We thank you that Jesus cared for the sick man
Altogether: God you are awesome!
(Blow bubbles.)
Finish with everyone saying together, 'God, you are awesome!'

AWESOME!

Sign 4

John 6:1–21

Aim To discover that Jesus fed a vast crowd when they were really hungry. Jesus knows about the ordinary things we need and he cares for us in practical ways.

Jesus cares for us in ways that matter

Jesus feeds 5,000 people

Notes for you

The crowds who followed Jesus were attracted to him as a healer and miracle worker, but didn't understand who he really was – the Son of God. As you explore these two stories with the children, pray that they will understand who Jesus is and how he knows them through and through. This means he can satisfy our deepest needs. He cares for us in real ways that do make a difference. This may be an alarming thought for some children but pray that as they find out about him during *Awesome!* they should be realising that Jesus can be trusted completely. What's more he wants us to become his followers.

Eye openers

Welcome the children to Awesome! If there are any newcomers, introduce yourself and any other adult helpers and make sure someone helps them complete a Flip-file or put on their Sparkling specs. If these are beginning to wear out, you may want to provide alternative forms of identity. Make sure that any child who has had a birthday since you last met is appropriately congratulated. As the children arrive, carry on making your Awesome! banner, if you have started to do so.

O1 Remember?
(5 minutes)

What you do
Ask if anyone can remember the three signs about Jesus that they have discovered so far – Jesus has God's power, can do the impossible and knows what's best for us. This might also be a good time to revise the Bible verses the children learned from the first two sessions – John 3:35 and Luke 18:27.

O2 Awesome! snack bar
(5–10 minutes)

What you need
- A table and awning set up as a snack bar (see Session 1)
- Fish fingers (one for each person)
- Tomato ketchup
- Hot dog rolls
- Paper plates (one for each person)
- Kitchen towel or paper serviettes

What you do
Unless it's really impossible to serve fish fingers, do have a go, as this will be something different and fun for the children. Perhaps some volunteers from your church could cook them at home and bring them to your venue wrapped in aluminium foil. Serve each fish finger inside a bread roll with tomato ketchup (like a hot dog). The children could help serve them. Alternatively you could serve picnic food such as sandwiches, crisps and sausages rolls.

Begin the meal by thanking God that he knows everything we need and provides for us.

O3 Yucky fish finger challenge!
(10 minutes)

You could do this while the children are finishing off their fish fingers, or before the children begin eating.

What you need
- At least two volunteers (leaders or confident older children)
- Fish fingers, newspaper, mashed potato (instant would be ideal), frying pans, hot dog rolls, tomato sauce, sticky tape, a clock with a second hand

What you do
Your leaders are going to see what they can do in one minute with a fish finger:
- Toss a fish finger in a frying pan as many times as possible in one minute.
- Make a mega fish finger roll, covered in tomato sauce and eat it within a minute.
- Wrap a fish finger in six separate pieces of newspaper, each piece stuck down with a piece of sticky tape.
- Find a fish finger hidden in a pile of mashed potato with their toes!

Divide the children into groups each supporting and cheering their leader!

O4 Bread and fishy races
(5–10 minutes)

What you need
- Materials for the race of your choice

What you do
As an alternative to 'Yucky fish finger challenge', devise races that involve everyone, such as an

42

JESUS CARES FOR US IN WAYS THAT MATTER

egg-and-spoon race using a fish finger on a spoon; or using a French stick to tap a balloon from one end of the room to the other – any team whose bread snaps in two is automatically out; or use a bread roll or tin of tuna as an object passed over the heads of a team etc.

◎5 Picnic food
(10–15 minutes)

What you need
- Rolled up newspapers to represent bread rolls (one per group)
- Fish shapes cut out of newspaper (one per group)

What you do
Split the children into small groups, each with an adult helper. Each group needs to stand in a row side by side and then sit down. Give a 'fish' and 'bread roll' to the person at one end of the row. There are two rules:
1 No one is allowed to touch the 'fish', but they can touch the 'bread roll'.
2 The 'fish' must be passed along the row by flapping it with the 'bread roll', creating a breeze to move it. When they have flapped the 'fish' enough to be in front of the next person in the row, the first person hands them the 'bread roll', and they continue the game.

The winning group is the quickest to pass the picnic food down their row and back again.

Fact finders

①1 Fish and bread
(5 minutes)

What you do
When Jesus went to a wedding, there was no wine left so he made some. This time Jesus provided food for a massive picnic. Awesome! Show the video clip *Fish and bread*.

①2 Read all about it!
(5 minutes)

What you need
- A copy of John's Gospel for each child, or a photocopy of the Bible verses on page 15 for each child (optional) for any who want to follow the story for themselves
- Volunteers to be Jesus, the boy and the crowd (with a leader for the crowd to imitate)

What you do
As you read John 6:3,5–15, your volunteers should do the following actions:
- The leader plus crowd walk towards Jesus, rubbing their stomachs with hunger.
- The small boy is brought to Jesus, holding a basket.
- The crowd sits down.
- Jesus holds up the bread.
- The crowd chews on their food and rubs satisfied stomachs.

Then talk about the second part of the story when Jesus came to his friends in the storm. You could adapt the following questions:
- The disciples had just seen Jesus feed a vast crowd. What do you think they would have been talking about as they got into the boat?
- If you'd been in the boat, how would you have felt when you saw what you thought was a ghost?
- What would they think of Jesus after this?
- Jesus knew his friends needed him. What things do you need? (Talk about the difference between wanting something and needing something.)
- Share your own experience of Jesus knowing what you needed and showing his care for you in real practical ways that made a difference.

Sign spotters

Choose from the following activities:

◎1 Action replay! part 2
(5–15 minutes)

What you need
- The photos from 'Action replay' in Session 3
- Large sheet of paper
- Glue stick and felt-tip pens
- White sticky labels and scissors to make speech bubbles

What you do
Show the children the photos from last session's 'Action replay!' Divide everyone into small groups, each with an adult helper. Give one or two photos to each group, along with a large sheet of paper, a glue stick and a felt-tip pen. The groups should stick the photos on the paper in order and add captions and speech bubbles for each one. It is important that the groups consult with each other before they write anything on the paper, so that the story flows properly. When everyone has finished, put the sheets together and display them. Read the

Checklist
- The children's Flip-files or Sparkling specs for them to use, plus spares for newcomers
- A copy of John's Gospel for each child, or a photocopy of the Bible verses on page 15 for each child (optional)
- Materials for your choice of activities for *Eye openers*, *Fact finders* and *Sign spotters*
- Materials for the *Awesome!* banner (see page 13)

When you see this logo, the activity is particularly appropriate for smaller groups.

When you see this logo, the activity will work well with older children.

43

photo story together. Comment on the fact that Jesus cared for the man in this story in ways that really mattered to him. Just as he did in this session's story

2 And the sign is…
(2 minutes)

What you do
Ask the children to tell you what you would need if…
you were ill?
you were tired?
you were dirty?
you were thirsty?
you were hungry?
Jesus knew what those people needed – a picnic! He showed his care for them in real ways that make a difference.

The fourth sign is:
Jesus cares for us in ways that matter. Awesome!

3 Jesus said…
(5 minutes)

What you need
- A very large speech bubble on which is written with a wax candle the words 'I am Jesus. Don't be afraid!' John 6:20
- Thick paint and a paintbrush

What you do
Lay the speech bubble down on a flat surface and ask a child to paint over the speech bubble. What are the hidden words? Ask everyone to read out what it says. Explain that this is what Jesus said when he knew his disciples were afraid. Move the bubble away and see if they can remember what Jesus said. (You could extend this activity by praying about things that make the group afraid.)

4 'What I need' box
(10 minutes)

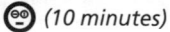

What you need
- Copies of the box template from page 26
- Pens, scissors and glue
- Straws cut up so that they fit into the little box
- Small pieces of paper

What you do
Give out copies of the box from page 26 and ask the children to cut out and make up the box. Give help as necessary to children who are struggling.

Ensure that the children know the difference between wanting something and needing it. On the small pieces of paper, encourage them to draw or write about something practical and genuine that they need, which may include something they need help with. Have some ideas ready as suggestions. It may be a specific object or something they are dreading in the future or something they are afraid of. They can draw/write about as many things as they can. Each piece of paper is screwed up into a tight roll and pushed into a straw, which is then put in the box. This is a secret between them and God. Have larger copies of the box and larger pieces of paper for younger children to use.

5 What's awesome?
(5 minutes)

What you need
- The children's Flip-files/Sparkling specs cases
- Felt-tip pens or pencils
- Pieces of paper small enough to fit inside the Flip-files/Sparkling specs cases

What you do
At the end of the session, encourage the children to think about what they remember most about today's programme and write or draw it on a piece of paper. Chat with the children as they work, and help as necessary. When they have finished, keep their pieces of paper safe in the child's Flip-file/Sparkling Specs case. Use this time to assess what the children have enjoyed and remembered. Is there anything you might want to do differently in the next session?

6 The Awesome! song
(5–10 minutes)

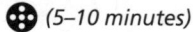

You will need
- The words to 'God is an awesome God' (see page 19)
- DVD player and the *Awesome!* DVD, or CD player and the CD *Light for Everyone*, or sheet music (see pages 20, 21) and piano/guitar

What you do
Finish your session by singing the *Awesome!* song. Go through the words and tune for any new children.

Awesome! prayers

Use one or both of these prayer ideas somewhere in your session.

What I need
(5 minutes)

What you need
- The 'What I need' boxes

What you do
Invite everyone to hold their box and think about what is inside. If Jesus could care for the disciples and the hungry crowd, he can help us. Be quiet for a moment and then thank God that he has heard all about our needs.

Speech bubbles
(5–10 minutes)

What you need
- A speech bubble shape for each child
- A basket
- Pens
- Envelopes

What you do
Give each child a speech bubble. Invite every child to write or draw a letter to God. It can be about anything. They may want to tell him how they are feeling. Perhaps they want to say, 'Thank you', ask him for something, or even say sorry. No one else will see the letters – they are private between each person and God. Of course, spelling and handwriting don't matter at all! Place each finished letter in an envelope, seal it and place it in the basket – a reminder of the boy who gave what he could to Jesus – five loaves and two fish. Encourage everyone to thank God silently that he knows about all the prayers that have been written in the letters and that he will answer each prayer in the best possible way.

Make sure you dispose of the letters after the session, or give them back to any children who would like to keep them in their Flip-file.

The children like the idea that spelling and handwriting don't matter too much when they're writing to God.

It meant a lot to one boy who wrote to God about his aunt who is ill.
Jean, Aldridge

AWESOME!

Sign 5

John 9:1–38

Aim To realise that the man whose sight had been restored gradually comes to understand who Jesus is – from man to prophet, then a man from God who is rejected, and finally Lord. Jesus came and still comes by his Spirit to help us understand God and become his friend.

Notes for you

In this miracle, the blind man whom Jesus healed also has his eyes opened to see who Jesus really is. He had lived in darkness until Jesus brought light into his life in two ways – the gift of sight and an understanding of Jesus as Lord. This is a long story (which has been shortened) and there are many themes which could be explored. However, at this stage in the *Awesome!* programme, the children's understanding of Jesus should be growing. This story is an important one to explore – who do they think Jesus is and what does he tell them about God?

Be sensitive about the issue of blindness. One group in the trial made direct connections with a girl who was blind, whom the children knew.

Pray for each child by name that they will see Jesus as their Lord and Saviour, and realise that, like the blind man, they can put their faith in him.

Jesus helps us understand God

Jesus heals a blind man

Eye openers

Welcome the children to Awesome! Ask anyone who has had a birthday this month to come out to the front. Light a birthday cake candle and invite everyone to sing 'Happy Birthday'. (This is to introduce the 'light' idea.) Alternatively, is there a local or national anniversary being celebrated this week? If so, mention that. Follow this with a few minutes of news and chat with the children. You could carry on creating your Awesome! banner as the children arrive.

01 Don't look!
(5–10 minutes)

What you need
- A blindfold
- Scrap paper and pens
- The following objects all hidden inside a large sock: an apple, a comb, a spoon, a paintbrush

What you do
Choose one or two volunteers to come to the front. Blindfold the volunteers and give them the sock to feel. After they have felt the sock, ask them to draw what they have felt while they are still wearing the blindfold. Show everyone the results and talk about how difficult it is to do anything when you can't see.

We put 10 objects in a pillow case which all the children felt and then everyone wrote them down. We didn't use a blindfold, although that would have made it more difficult.
Rosey, Sutton

We sat in four circles with a leader and every child took part. We used pillowslips to fit in more objects. We stayed in these circles for several other activities in this session.
Rosemary, Gorgie

02 Seeing and not seeing
(5–10 minutes)

Several variations are suggested for this.

What you need
- Enough blindfolds for one between three
- Four foods for tasting (be aware of food allergies)
- Objects to make a simple obstacle course

What you do
a) Divide the children into groups of two or three, making sure no one is left out. One child puts on the blindfold, while the other one or two children act as guides. They should lead the blindfolded person around the room. If lots of children are doing this at the same time, they need to avoid each other. Swap over after a few minutes. When everyone has had a turn, the small groups should discuss the questions below.
b) Older children can give each other verbal instructions to go blindfold round a simple obstacle course.
c) One blindfolded child is fed different foods by another. This requires trust and can be quite isolating for the blindfolded child. You could do this as part of your refreshments.

■ DISCUSSION QUESTIONS
- How did it feel to be blindfolded?
- What couldn't you do if you were blind?
- What was the worst thing about not being able to see?
- Were you frightened of anything when you couldn't see? If so, what?
- How do blind people manage? What different things help them?
- How might it feel if you'd been blind since you were born but suddenly you discovered you could see? What would you think of your family or what you looked like or trees, buses and colours?

46

JESUS HELPS US UNDERSTAND GOD

Those who were fed really needed to trust those who were feeding them especially as there were sprouts on offer!
Jean, Aldridge

We had to be sensitive as there was a girl in the school who's blind. We related this to her – how might she feel if you're all pushing to the front and she was in the middle?
Rosey, Sutton

⊙3 Awesome! snack bar
(5–15 minutes)

What you need:
- A table and awning set up as a snack bar (see Session 1)
- Snack food and drinks
- Slices of bread (or toast) with different toppings, such as cheese spread, honey, Marmite, and different flavours of jam (avoid peanut butter and chocolate hazelnut spread in case of allergies)
- Blindfolds and clean-up facilities, if you are doing blindfold feeding

What you do
Serve the children with food and drinks. Encourage the adult helpers to chat with the children while you have your refreshments. If you are doing blindfold feeding here, get some volunteers to be blindfolded and fed!

Fact finders

①1 The blind man
(5 minutes)

What you do
Some people go blind when they are old, or as the result of an accident. Jesus met a man who had been born blind. Show the video clip *The blind man*.

①2 Read all about it!
(5 minutes)

What you need:
- A copy of John's Gospel for each child, or a photocopy of the Bible verses on page 16 for each child (optional)
- Large copy of John 9:1–38 from page 16
- The pictures from page 16 enlarged and put on a flip chart or OHP acetate, or a leader who is prepared to act out the part of the blind man, with appropriate props

What you do
A leader sits at the front blindfold. As a competent reader reads the story, the leader mimes the actions. (Another leader will need to put mud on the eyes, accompanied by suitable yuks!) He looks puzzled though whenever he is asked questions about Jesus. Draw attention to his growing understanding of who Jesus is.

Alternatively, photocopy and enlarge the pictures down the side of the Bible passage and make them into a strip of film or put on a flip chart, to reveal as the story is read.

Sign spotters

Choose from the following activities:

①1 Oh, I see!
(10–15 minutes)

What you do
Ask the children if they have ever been in a situation where they have said, 'Oh, I see!' Perhaps they were at school trying to get their brain around a difficult sum! Were they blind and then suddenly got their sight back? No, of course not! What did they really mean when they said, 'Oh, I see!'?

In twos or threes, ask the children to act out a short scene in which the punchline is 'Oh, I see!' For example, a child is trying to change a burst tyre on their bicycle and getting in a mess until someone comes to show them how to do it. Or someone is lost until they are given a map of where to go. If there's time, invite each group to show everyone else their sketch.

Talk about how the blind man in the story began to see and understand more and more of who Jesus is. Adapt these questions to guide the discussion.

Imagine that, like this blind man, you had been blind from birth and a beggar whom no one took seriously. What would you know about Jesus before you met him?

What did the blind man know about Jesus after he had been healed?

What was important when the man called Jesus 'Lord' and worshipped him? (Think how you will explain this to the children.)

Checklist
- The children's Flip-files or Sparkling specs for them to use, plus spares for newcomers
- A copy of John's Gospel for each child, or a photocopy of the Bible verses on page 16 for each child (optional)
- Materials for your choice of activities for *Eye openers*, *Fact finders* and *Sign spotters*
- Materials for the *Awesome!* banner (see page 13)

⊕ *When you see this logo, the activity is particularly appropriate for smaller groups.*

☺ *When you see this logo, the activity will work well with older children.*

5

47

AWESOME!

5

And the fifth sign is:
Jesus helps us understand God! Awesome!

When I asked who was really being blind in today's story, someone immediately said, 'The Pharisees'!
Jean, Aldridge

2 Braille messages
(10–15 minutes)

What you need
- Sheets of card, marked up as shown
- Split pins
- Copies of the Braille alphabet (type 'Braille alphabet' into an Internet search engine)

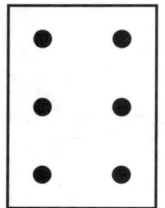

Mark up the card with a series of these boxes like this one, so that the children can see where to push the split-pins.

What you do
Show the children how to push the split pins through the card to spell the word 'Jesus' or 'Light' or 'Awesome'. They could do their name or their football team. As you do this, you could explore how the blind man's understanding grew using the three questions at the end of 'Oh! I see!' above.

For a cheaper and easier activity for younger hands, you could use small, round, glitter stickers on card marked with dots.

Everyone, except one boy who wasn't in the mood to enjoy anything, really enjoyed this. It did use rather a lot of split pins though!
Jean, Aldridge

3 Glass painting
(10–15 minutes)

What you need
- A jam jar or glass for each child
- A tea light for each child
- Glass paints, brushes and stickers

What you do
Encourage each child to paint a pattern on the glass. When they have finished, give them a tea light to put inside their jar. While everyone is working, use the questions in *Sign spotters* 'Oh, I see!' to guide the discussion as you paint.

The girls enjoyed this and the parents were appreciative too. The girls were pleased to take these home.
Chris, Croxley

4 What's awesome?
(5 minutes)

What you need
- The children's Flip-files/Sparkling specs cases
- Felt-tip pens or pencils
- Pieces of paper small enough to fit inside the Flip-files/Sparkling specs cases

What you do
At the end of the session, encourage the children to think about what they remember most about today's programme and write or draw it on a piece of paper. Chat with the children as they work, and help as necessary. When they have finished, keep their pieces of paper safe in the child's Flip-file/Sparkling specs case. How are the children enjoying the club so far? Are there any children whom you might specifically pray for, following what the children have said?

5 The Awesome! song
(5–10 minutes)

You will need
- The words to 'God is an awesome God' (see page 19)
- DVD player and the *Awesome!* DVD, or CD player and the CD *Light for Everyone*, or sheet music (see pages 20, 21) and piano/guitar

What you do
Finish your session by singing the *Awesome!* song.

Awesome! prayers

Use one or both of these prayer ideas somewhere in your session.
(5 minutes)

Light prayers

What you need
- A tea light for each person, or one big candle
- A tin lid or flat container to hold the small candles
- Matches (optional)

What you do
Make sure you take steps to ensure the safety of everyone in your group if you decide to light candles. Make sure you have assessed all the risks and put in place any necessary safety measures.

Give each person their tea light. Ask them to hold it and sit in a space on the floor. If you have enough adult helpers, you could light the tea lights and place them on the flat container in the centre, but it is not essential. Alternatively, light your large candle. The candles remind us of something Jesus said to the blind man:

> 'I am the light for the world.'

He came to help us understand God. Ask everyone to repeat after you: 'Jesus came to help us understand God.'

Explain that you will say some short prayers. When you say, 'Thank you, God, because…', the children can respond with the words, 'Jesus came to help us understand you.'

Thank you, God, for your power. Thank you that your power healed the blind man.
Thank you, God, because…
Thank you, God, because you can do things that are impossible for anyone else.
Thank you, God, because…
Thank you, God, that when Jesus told the blind man to go and wash, the blind man realised that Jesus knows what's best for us.
Thank you, God, because…
Thank you, God, that Jesus cares for us in ways that matter.
Thank you, God, because…
Please God, help us be like the blind man and understand more about you.

If you have lit any candles, everyone could blow them out together at the end of the prayer.

Light/dark prayers

What you need
- Someone to lower the lighting as appropriate

What you do
Sit round in a circle. Encourage as many children as you can to share something that puzzles them, such as why some people have food and others don't, what school they might go to next year.

As the helper turns down the lights, tell God about these things.

Turn up the lights again, and thank God that, although we cannot understand everything, we know that God understands and he helps us when we are puzzled. Conclude with everyone saying the phrase, 'We all know that Jesus helps us understand God!'

AWESOME!

Sign 6

John 11:1–44

Aim To recognise that Jesus had such power that he could bring someone back to life. Jesus is able to comfort us in sadness and can give us new life on earth and in heaven.

Notes for you

Although they didn't realise it at the time, when Jesus raised Lazarus from the tomb, he was showing the people what would happen when God brought his own Son back to life. This final, powerful sign was the ultimate proof that Jesus has God's power over death and gives hope and new life. Think about how you will explain the new life that Jesus gives to us now and into eternity. Pray that the children will understand that they too can have life with God that starts now and goes on forever.

Some children may be facing bereavement, so be especially sensitive to them. How will you explain death and heaven to them? Children may have all sorts of ideas about heaven and death! Be prepared, too, for questions about the destiny of the pet rabbit!

Jesus gives new life

Eye openers

Welcome the children to Awesome! Ask everyone to get into small groups with an adult helper. Invite them to catch up with each other and share any news they have. If you have been making the Awesome! banner in previous sessions, carry on with it as the children arrive.

O1 Make a mummy
(5–10 minutes)

What you need
- A white toilet roll for each small group, plus a spare roll to use later
- A bin liner to collect the rubbish

What you do
Explain that when someone died in the first century AD, their body was wrapped in linen cloths a bit like bandages. Then it was placed in a cave with a large stone rolled across the entrance to seal it.

Split the children into small groups, with an adult leader in every group. Give each team a toilet roll. Ask them to mummify the smallest person in their group (provided that they are willing) by wrapping the toilet roll around them, like a bandage. When the groups have finished, inspect each 'mummy' and, if appropriate, decide on the best as the winner. Unwrap the mummies and collect the rubbish in a bin liner.

Explain that in this story Jesus went to the home of two sisters called Martha and Mary, and also to the cave where the body of their brother Lazarus was buried.

We gave a prize for the neatest, the quickest and the mummy with the most potential! The children really enjoyed this!
Rosey, Sutton

Jesus raises Lazarus from the dead

O2 Hoop games
(5–10 minutes)

You will need
- Enough hoops for each team of children
- Beanbags or some other objects to throw into the hoop

What you do
There are several games involving hoops which you could play:

1 In teams, the children race each other from one point to another, rolling the hoop. You could create an obstacle course to make this more difficult. (This could be done with a ball, rolled along the ground.)

2 In teams, the first child runs from one end of a room to the other, dropping a beanbag into the hoop on the way. The second child picks the beanbag up and so on.

3 Time how long children can keep a hoop circling around their waist. Who is the winner? (Bounce a ball instead of hula-hooping.)

Introduce the idea that when people were buried at the time of Jesus they were put into a cave and a stone was rolled across the entrance, which features in this session's story.

O3 Awesome! snack bar
(5–15 minutes)

What you need
- A table and awning set up as a snack bar (see Session 1)
- Paper serviettes
- Food for a simple buffet, such as sausage rolls, crisps, cubes of cheese and chocolate biscuits

What you do
Invite the children to choose one of each item from the buffet and wrap it up in the serviette, like a mummy. Thank God for the food and, at a given sign, the children can unwrap their food and eat it! Make sure adult helpers chat with the children while you are eating.

JESUS GIVES NEW LIFE

😊 *We made popcorn and talked about how the popcorn was changed. Then we ate it. Great fun and very messy!* 😊
Rosey, Sutton

Fact finders

▶1 Lazarus
✳ 😊 *(5 minutes)*

What you do
Jesus didn't arrive at Mary and Martha's house until after their brother Lazarus had died. Was it too late? Show the video clip *Lazarus*.

▶2 Read all about it!
✳ 😊 *(10 minutes)*

What you do
Practise doing a thumbs up and a thumbs down when you give the children some good or some bad news. For example, school is cancelled for the week, ice cream is free for the day. Include some news which could be either such as, it's been very hot all week and now it is raining!

Invite a leader to read parts of John 11:1–44 slowly and dramatically.

Verses 1a, 3, 4–8, 17–44 – the reader should pause after the following verses: 3, 4, 6, 17, 19, 21, 23, 26, 29, 35, 39, 44. After each pause, ask the children to do a thumbs up or down and discuss whether it was good news, bad news or a bit of both!

Sign spotters

Choose from the following activities:

●1 Grass heads
✳ *(10 minutes)*

What you need
- Grass seeds
- Popsocks or old tights
- Sawdust
- Permanent marker pens, elastic bands, glue
- Felt

What you do
Put a few grass seeds at the bottom of a sock and fill the rest of the space with sawdust. Tie a knot at the top. Stick on wiggly felt eyes, draw a mouth with a marker pen and create a nose and ears with elastic bands. Sprinkle a little water on the grass seeds. (Prepare one before the session, so the children know what they are aiming at.)

These seeds will spring into new life. Discuss what new life meant for Lazarus. You may want to adapt the following questions:
- What do you think Lazarus and his sisters thought about Jesus when he didn't come to help them?
- What do you think everyone there thought when they saw Jesus crying?
- What do you think everyone thought about Jesus when they saw Lazarus walk out of the tomb? What sort of a person does that make Jesus?
- What sort of things have made you feel sad recently?
- Do you think Jesus could understand all about it?
- (Use only if appropriate.) How do you feel when someone you love has died?

Jesus gave Lazarus a new life. How can Jesus give us a new life which doesn't have to wait until we have died? (Be prepared to share your own experience of this.)

You may need to mention that Jesus came alive himself but, for children outside the church, the resurrection may be something unknown to them. They will hear about this in session 7.

😊 *At the moment the grass seeds look dead, but soaked in water, green hair should start to grow profusely!* 😊
Jean, Aldridge

●2 Stone painting
✳ 😊 *(5–10 minutes)*

You will need
- A flat stone for each child
- Paint and brushes

What you do
Show the children how to create bright, full-of-life patterns on their stones. As you all work, talk about the stone that was rolled away from Lazarus' tomb and the new life he received. You could use the questions in 'Grass heads'.

Checklist
- The children's Flip-files or Sparkling specs for them to use, plus spares for newcomers
- A copy of John's Gospel for each child, or a photocopy of the Bible verses on page 17 for each child (optional)
- Materials for your choice of activities for *Eye openers*, *Fact finders* and *Sign spotters*
- Materials for the *Awesome!* banner (see page 13)

✳ *When you see this logo, the activity is particularly appropriate for smaller groups.*

😊 *When you see this logo, the activity will work well with older children.*

51

3 Bad news, good news
(5 minutes)

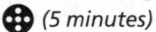

What you do
Go back over the *Awesome!* stories and think how many of them began with bad news, like the news that Lazarus had died, but finished as good news, as Jesus raised Lazarus from the dead. Use this as an opportunity to remind the children of the six *Awesome!* signs about Jesus.

4 And the sign is…
(5–10 minutes)

What you need
- A large, rough circle cut from a sheet of brown wrapping paper to represent the tombstone
- A felt-tip pen
- Bibles to share

What you do
Attach the 'tombstone' to the wall. Use the questions from 'Grass heads' and write any key words or phrases on it as the children respond to the questions.

Remove the 'tombstone' and turn it over to show the blank side. Invite the children to get into twos and threes and find John 11:25. Ask someone to read it aloud slowly while you write the words on the reverse of the 'tombstone' – 'Jesus said, "I am the one who raises the dead to life! Everyone who has faith in me will live, even if they die."' Say the verse together several times.

Explain how Jesus gave Lazarus new life. He wants to give us new life too. And it's life that starts now but goes on after we die, when we will be with God in heaven forever. Awesome!
The sixth sign is:
Jesus gives new life. Awesome!

5 My new life
(5–10 minutes)

What you do
Invite one of the adult helpers (or someone from your church known to the children) to give a brief, simple testimony of the new life that Jesus has given him or her. If appropriate, allow a few minutes at the end for the children to ask questions.

6 What's awesome?
(5 minutes)

What you need
- The children's Flip-files/Sparkling specs cases
- Felt-tip pens or pencils
- Pieces of paper small enough to fit inside the Flip-files/Sparkling specs cases

What you do
At the end of the session, encourage the children to think about what they remember most about today's programme and write or draw it on a piece of paper. Chat with the children as they work, and help as necessary. When they have finished, keep their pieces of paper safe in the child's Flip-file/Sparkling Specs case. How are the children enjoying the club so far? Are there any children who you might specifically pray for, following what the children have said?

It's important that the children have an opportunity to talk about death.
Cheryl, Cardiff

JESUS GIVES NEW LIFE

Awesome! prayers

Use one or both of these prayer ideas somewhere in your session.
(5 minutes)

Thumbs up and down

What you do
Sit round in a circle (or if a large group break into smaller circles.) Everyone puts their thumbs down as you mention people who are sad. If necessary, the leader writes down all their names. Then everyone turns their thumbs up and the leader thanks God that Jesus comforts those who are sad and he understands. Pray for each sad person by name. If the children want to pray out loud, or just mention a name themselves, then encourage them to do so.

Singing prayers

What you need
- The *Light for Everyone* CD and means of playing track 11, 'God is an awesome God'

What you do
Everyone joins in the song, thinking about the line, 'He gives new life, this is what he said, follow me!' Ask God out loud that each child will discover what it means to receive Jesus' new life.

AWESOME!

Sign 7

John 20:1–18; 21:1–14

Aim To help the children grasp that Jesus died, but he came alive again, not as a spooky ghost, but as someone who makes breakfast for his friends and calls them by name. Those children who are spiritually prepared might start to consider how Jesus relates to them in a similar way today.

Notes for you

In this ultimate miracle, God raised Jesus to life, having conquered sin and death once and for all. This is the good news we are sharing with the children. Pray that they will respond to God's love and saving power. But remember that children can have strange ideas about death and ghosts. Be prepared to talk about emotions and how you personally respond to the fact that Jesus is alive.

This is a story with two distinctive components: Mary's encounter with Jesus and the breakfast on the beach. You may wish to only concentrate on one of them.

Jesus is alive for ever!

Eye openers

Welcome the children to Awesome! Ask everyone to get into small groups with an adult helper. Invite them to tell each other what their favourite time of year is, and why. As the children arrive, finish off your Awesome! banner, if you have been doing it.

O1 Easter egg hunt
(5–10 minutes)

What you need
- Small pictures of Easter eggs
- Small Easter eggs (or alternative)

What you do
Before the session, hide the pictures of Easter eggs around the room. Set a time limit and invite the children to go on an Easter egg hunt. They can find three pictures each and then help someone else find their three pictures. At the end of the session, they can swap their pictures for an Easter egg, but make sure you keep the pictures in a safe place! Some children may not like Easter eggs, so have an alternative available.

You could do this with real Easter eggs or other sweets, but some children are likely to find more than their fair share. If the shops do not have Easter eggs because it is the wrong time of year, use other sweets.

When the time is up, ask what ideas the word 'Easter' gives the children. For most people, Easter is about hot cross buns and chocolate eggs, but for Christians, the really important part of Easter is about something else.

O2 Egg games
(10 minutes)

What you do
Devise a variety of hard-boiled egg games and races, although you might prefer to use potatoes instead. For example, an egg-and-spoon race, rolling a potato/egg through and around a series of obstacles.

Jesus is raised to life

Lead a discussion from what time of the year we think of eggs, to the Easter story.

O3 Eggshell butterflies
(5–10 minutes)

What you need
- Clean eggshells, washed and crushed into smallish pieces
- Different colours of food colouring
- An enlarged copy of the butterfly template from page 27 for each child
- Glue, scissors

What you do
Before the session, break the eggshells into very small pieces and colour them by placing them in diluted food colouring.

Give each child an enlarged copy of the butterfly on page 27. The children should spread glue over their butterfly, then sprinkle different coloured eggshell fragments on top. Press gently to ensure they are stuck and shake off any excess. If it is near Easter time, these could be stuck on card to make Easter cards.

Talk about when we think about new life and butterflies and link that into a discussion about what happens in the spring, leading on to Easter.

O4 Awesome! snack bar
(5–15 minutes)

What you need
- A table and awning set up as a snack bar (see Session 1)
- Breakfast food, such as juice, cereal and milk, toast or bread rolls with butter or margarine and jam
- A 'Surprise breakfast' menu, written on a blackboard or a large piece of paper (optional)

What you do
Explain that they are going to have a surprise breakfast, even though it is (time of day)! Show everyone the menu. Helpers can act as waiters

and take orders from each child, then serve them with their surprise breakfast. This leads on to the surprise breakfast that Jesus gave his disciples.

05 Where are we?
(5 minutes)

What you need
- An empty shoebox
- An envelope
- An empty suitcase
- An empty tube of Smarties

What you do
Choose four confident children to come to the front. Explain that you are about to show them something completely awesome! Give each child one of the items. Make a great show of asking each child to look inside their item and reveal what is there to everyone. When each child in turn says that there is nothing, exclaim how wonderful it is that the box, envelope, case or tube is empty!

Then acknowledge that of course it isn't particularly wonderful. But there was something amazing about something that was empty in this session's story. What was so awesome about the fact that it was empty? Ask the children to look out for at least two empty things in the video (the cave/tomb and the disciples' nets).

Fact finders

01 Dead or alive?
(5 minutes)

What you do
Follow straight on from *Eye openers* 'Where are we?' and show the video clip *Dead or alive?* without further comment.

02 Read all about it!
(10–15 minutes)

What you need:
- A copy of John's Gospel for each child, or a photocopy of the Bible verses on page 18
- The appropriate number of volunteers (helpers or children) for the option you have chosen

What you do
One leader reads John 20:11–18, while competent readers can follow it in their own copy of the verses. Four volunteers act out the parts of Mary, the angels and Jesus. They may need to rehearse this in advance.

Follow this up by adapting some of these questions:
- How would you feel if your best friend, or someone you really loved, had gone away?
- If appropriate, explore how they would feel if such a person had died.
- What would you do to show you loved them?
- How would you then feel if they turned up again, quite unexpectedly? That it was a dream? That you were seeing things?
- Why do you think Mary did not recognise Jesus and his voice?
- What do you think had happened to Jesus?
- What do you think Mary felt then?
- Why is this such an awesome thing to happen?

One leader reads John 21:1–14, while competent readers can follow it in their own copy of the verses. Four volunteers act out the parts of Peter, Jesus and at least two disciples. They may need to rehearse this in advance. Note that the children will not necessarily know the story where Peter has let Jesus down since that has not been covered in *Awesome!* This story stops before Jesus speaks alone with Peter.

Follow this up by adapting some of these questions:
- What sort of people work at night? *(Add 'fishermen' if this is not suggested.)*
- Why do people fish at night?
- How do you think Jesus' disciples felt after a night of fishing without catching anything?
- And how might they have felt after they caught all these fish?
- Can anyone remember how many there were? *(153)*
- How might Peter have felt when he realised it was Jesus on the beach? Was Jesus a ghost?
- How did Jesus show his disciples that he was an ordinary man and still cared for them?
- How is the fact that Jesus came alive again such an awesome thing? What does that say about Jesus?

❝ One child said it just wasn't fair what they did to Jesus. ❞
Cheryl, Cardiff

Checklist
- The children's Flip-files or Sparkling specs for them to use, plus spares for newcomers
- A copy of John's Gospel for each child, or a photocopy of the Bible verses on page 18 for each child (optional)
- Materials for your choice of activities for *Eye openers*, *Fact finders* and *Sign spotters*
- Materials for the *Awesome!* banner (see page 13)

When you see this logo, the activity is particularly appropriate for smaller groups.

When you see this logo, the activity will work well with older children.

Sign spotters

Choose from the following activities:

1 Easter cards
(10 minutes)

If it is approaching Easter when you do this session, this activity would be especially appropriate.

What you need
- Card and the stone illustration from page 27, copied onto card
- Split pins
- Felt-tip pens, scissors

What you do
Prepare the cards and stones as shown on page 27. (For younger children, do this in advance.) Attach the stone to the card with a split pin as shown. The stone can then be rolled away again. Inside the card, the children should write the message, JESUS IS RISEN, so that when the stone is rolled back, the words can be read inside the tomb.

As you make these, talk about what it means to you that Jesus is alive and not dead.

2 Rolling stone, iced biscuits
(5–10 minutes)

What you need
- Plain, round biscuits
- Pre-prepared icing and sugar strands etc

What you do
Give each child a biscuit and encourage them to decorate it as they wish. As everyone is working, talk about the stone being rolled away from the tomb and what that meant about Jesus being alive again. Try to ensure that you can share what it means to you that Jesus is alive.

3 And the sign is…
(5 minutes)

What you need
- The phrase 'Jesus is alive for ever!' written in large bubble writing
- Felt-tip pens

What you do
Divide the children into four groups, with mixed ages/colouring ability in each group and set them the task of colouring in or decorating four letters each, including a 'bubble' exclamation mark. They have just five minutes. Display their handiwork on a board for all to see.

The seventh sign is:
Jesus is alive for ever! Awesome!

4 What's awesome?
(5 minutes)

What you need
- The children's Flip-files/Sparkling specs cases
- Felt-tip pens or pencils
- Pieces of paper small enough to fit inside the Flip-files/Sparkling specs cases

What you do
At the end of the session, encourage the children to think about what they remember most about today's programme and write or draw it on a piece of paper. Chat with the children as they work, and help as necessary. When they have finished, keep their pieces of paper safe in the child's Flip-file/Sparkling Specs case. You might be able to assess what impact the teaching has had on the children. Can you identify any prayer needs from what the children remember and say?

5 The Awesome! song
(5–10 minutes)

What you need
- The words to 'God is an awesome God' (see page 19)
- DVD player and the *Awesome!* DVD, or CD player and the CD *Light for Everyone*, or sheet music (see pages 20, 21) and piano/guitar

What you do
Finish your session by singing the *Awesome!* song. Sing it through a couple of times if the children are enjoying themselves.

This was a particularly difficult evening. It reminds us that our message is a powerful one and we are in a spiritual battle. We need to pray so much for our children. Some of them are struggling with so much 'baggage'.

Jean, Aldridge

Awesome! prayer

Use one or both of these prayer ideas somewhere in your session.

The seven signs
(3 minutes)

What you need
- The seven signs from the previous weeks, written out

What you do
Ask everyone to listen while you pray and thank God for the seven signs that show us more about Jesus. Read through the list of signs slowly, saying 'Thank you, God, because Jesus…' before each one. Invite anyone who agrees with what you have prayed to say 'Amen' as a way of making it their prayer too.

Stone prayers
(5 minutes)

What you need
- A stone

What you do
Sit the children in a circle. Begin your prayer with the words, 'Thank you, Jesus, that you are alive forever.' Pass the stone round and invite each child, when they are holding it, to finish off this sentence:

Thank you, Jesus, that you are with me at/in _____

The children might say school, home or the night-time. If you do not have a stone, use another appropriate object. Children who do not want to do this can just pass the stone on to the next child. If you have a larger group, split the children into smaller groups.

Sign 8
John 20:30,31

What about us?

Aim To review Awesome! and leave the children keen to discover more. Also to encourage each child to make a (further) step in their commitment to follow Jesus. You may want to invite parents to join you at some stage of the session.

Notes for you
The Bible verses summarise the aim of John's Gospel – that its readers might believe that Jesus is the promised Saviour, the Son of God, and that through faith in him they might have life. You may need to remind the children what Messiah means. How would you put verses 30 and 31 in your own words in explaining them to a child? There is no new story today but many stories will feature. You may prefer to concentrate on reviewing just one. It could be that there was one session which did not go especially well for you. Look back at the material and see if you could take ideas you have not used already. But don't lose sight of the need to take an overview of the whole series to emphasise that Jesus is awesome and wants to have a relationship with each one of us.
Pray that each child will respond to what they have learned during *Awesome!* and accept the life that God offers them through Jesus. There are guidelines for helping children respond on page 8.

Eye openers

As the children arrive, welcome them to the final Awesome! session. Show them the Awesome! banner or poster that they have made together and congratulate them on their hard work. Some children could decorate a cake to celebrate your Awesome! club, which you can share later in the session. Choose a selection of the following activities, depending on the time you have available.

☺ *The children enjoyed making a seven signs banner when they first arrived.* ☺
Chris, Croxley Green

◎1 Hat-making
(10–15 minutes)

What you need
- Two large sheets of newspaper for each child
- Scissors, staplers and sticky tape
- Coloured crêpe paper cut into thin strips (enough for two per child)

What you do
Explain that the final *Awesome!* session is a party to celebrate how awesome Jesus is.
Challenge everyone to see who can make the most awesome party hat. Give each person two sheets of paper and two strips of coloured crêpe paper. Make sure adult helpers are available to offer assistance. Allow everyone a time limit. When the time is up, have a parade of the hats, and if appropriate, declare which hat is the most awesome and therefore, the winner. You could have other prizes such as one for the oddest, the most carefully made, the smallest etc.
With older children, you could introduce more sophisticated materials or templates. For example, you could give each child a forehead band, to which they could attach ears, nose, hair and all sorts of other 'shapes'. Alternatively, ask them to select a character from *Awesome!* and create a hat suitable for that person.
As you work together on this, talk about what children have remembered and enjoyed about the *Awesome!* programme.

Final sign-up

☺ *The hat-making went well and lots of the hats really were awesome!* ☺
Jean, Aldridge

◎2 Old favourites
(20–40 minutes)

Have a re-run of some of the *Awesome!* activities and games from the previous sessions that the children really enjoyed. Bear in mind that parents may be watching or even joining in. Before you introduce each activity, remind the children what it was about.. Here are some suggestions:
Water game (Session 1)
Possible or impossible? (Session 2)
Races without legs (Session 3)
Picnic food (Session 4)
Don't look! (Session 5)
Easter egg hunt (Session 7)

◎3 Awesome! snack bar
(5–10 minutes)

What you need
- A table and awning set up as a snack bar (see Session 1)
- Party food
- Christian CDs playing as background music

What you do
Serve the party food to the children. You might even have an *Awesome!* cake (ready made, and decorated by the children at the start of the session). If appropriate, give a public vote of thanks to those responsible for the *Awesome!* snack bar.

58

Fact finders

①1 Balloon bonanza
(10 minutes)

What you need
- The following words written on a large sheet of paper and cut into ten strips as follows: These are written / so that you will / put your faith / in Jesus / the Son of God. / If you have / faith in him / you will have / true life / John 20:31
- Ten balloons
- A pencil
- A Bible (Contemporary English Version – if you have another version, amend the text of the memory verse accordingly)

What you do
Cut the paper into strips where indicated. Wrap each strip around the pencil then push it inside a balloon. Inflate the balloons and tie a knot in each one. Ask the children the following questions and at the point indicated, a child bursts a balloon. Retrieve the slips of paper inside and ask the children to help you arrange the words in the correct order. Check the verse in the Bible and then read it together several times. Talk about what it means to put your faith in Jesus (see 'What about us?' in *Sign spotters*).

- What went wrong at the wedding Jesus went to? *(The wine ran out.)*
- And what did Jesus do about it? *(Turned six huge jars full of water into the best wine possible.)*

Pop a balloon!
- What went wrong in the home of the prince? *(His son was dying.)*
- And what did Jesus do about it? *(Jesus healed him without even going to see him.)*

Pop a balloon!
- What are the first and the second signs?

Pop a balloon!
- What had gone wrong for the lame man by the pool? *(He couldn't walk. He could never get near enough to the pool to get in and be healed.)*
- And what did Jesus do about it? *(He healed him.)*

Pop a balloon!
- What went wrong for the crowd of people listening to Jesus? *(It got late, they were far from home and there was no food.)*
- And what did Jesus do about it? *(He fed them all.)*

Pop a balloon!

- What are the third and fourth signs?

Pop a balloon!
- What happened to the blind man after Jesus healed him? *(The Jewish leaders threw him out of the temple/meeting place.)*
- And what did Jesus do about it? *(Jesus found him and the man trusted Jesus.)*

Pop a balloon!
- What went wrong for Lazarus' two sisters? *(Their brother was ill, Jesus didn't come and then Lazarus died.)*
- And what did Jesus do about it? *(He came, comforted the sisters and raised Lazarus to life.)*

Pop a balloon!
- What went wrong when Jesus' enemies arrested Jesus? *(He was put on trial and killed.)*
- And what did Jesus do about it? *(He came alive again. He couldn't stay dead. He met with his friends, Mary, Peter and the others.)*

Pop a balloon!
- What are the fifth, sixth and seventh signs?

Pop a balloon!

①2 Slogan shout
(5 minutes)

What you need
- The *Awesome!* banner, if you made it (optional)

What you do
Call out each of the signs from the sessions in order, but stop before the end so that the children can supply the missing words. For example, you say, 'Jesus has…' and the children call out, '…God's power'.

Sign spotters

Choose from the following activities:

①1 What about us?
(5 minutes)

What you need
- A simple leaflet about becoming a Christian for each child, see page 10 (this may not be appropriate for every child, but have a few available)

What you do
Ask the children the following questions. Depending on the type of group you have, it may be more appropriate to ask them to think

Checklist
- Your *Awesome!* banner on display, if you made one
- Decorations to create a party atmosphere, such as balloons, streamers and party hats
- The children's Flip-files or Sparkling specs for them to use
- A copy of John's Gospel for each child, or a photocopy of the Bible verses on page 17 for each child (optional)
- Materials for your choice of activities for *Eye openers*, *Fact finders* and *Sign spotters*
- Details of what your club is doing next, plus any future events
- A simple leaflet about becoming a Christian – see page 10 (this may not be appropriate for every child, but have a few available)

When you see this logo, the activity is particularly appropriate for smaller groups.

When you see this logo, the activity will work well with older children.

about the answers rather than calling them out or putting up their hand:
- What do the signs tell us about who Jesus is?
- How could Jesus make a difference in your life? (Be prepared to share what it means to you to follow Jesus.)

Explain that Jesus came to give us life that starts now and never ends, because one day we will be in heaven with God forever! If we ask Jesus to give us a new start, he will. Give anyone who wants to know more about this the opportunity to chat with you afterwards. (If you have leaflets or booklets available you could offer these to anyone who is interested.)

> *One child suddenly asked what happened to Jesus after his resurrection. 'Did he live peacefully and die of old age at the end?' A reminder that we do need to mention the ascension at some point! I've often met children who happily accept that Jesus came alive again but assume that he then had to die again (as Lazarus did) before going to heaven.*
> Jean, Aldridge

If the children would benefit from hearing about Jesus' ascension into heaven, do fill in details of the final stage of Jesus' life on earth, reading Acts 1:1–11.

2 What's awesome?
(5 minutes)

What you need
- The children's Flip-files/Sparkling specs cases
- Felt-tip pens or pencils
- Pieces of paper small enough to fit inside the Flip-files/Sparkling specs cases

What you do
In this final session, invite the children to write about or draw what they most remember, what they most enjoyed or what most surprised them from all the *Awesome!* sessions they have been to.

Don't forget!
Give each child his or her Flip-file or Sparkling specs case to take home. Encourage the children to come along to other activities you have planned. It would be worth sending such information home to parents and carers.

As a team of leaders, conclude the series together by praising God that he is awesome and has done awesome things in the lives of each child who has attended. Ask him to complete what he has begun!

Awesome! prayers

Use one or both of these prayer ideas somewhere in your session
(5–10 minutes)

Speech bubble praise

What you need
- A large sheet of paper
- Several thick felt-tip pens

What you do
Ask everyone to sit in a large circle. Place the sheet of paper on the floor and draw a huge speech bubble. Invite anyone who wants to, to call out what they would like to say to our awesome God. They could be single words of praise and thanks, or phrases, or short sentences. As different people call things out, write or draw them in the speech bubble. If you have a big group and lots of suggestions, adult leaders could use the spare pens to help with the writing. Pray, mentioning as many of the words and phrases that you can. Finish by encouraging everyone to repeat after you, 'We praise you God, because you are awesome!' Sing the *Awesome!* song to finish.

Parachute prayers

What you need
- A parachute

What you do
Each child takes it in turns to say, 'Thank you, God, for _____'. Between each prayer, lift the parachute and call out 'We praise you God because you are awesome!' Sing the *Awesome!* song to finish.

AWESOME!

Books
to help you

Jesus and the starving crowd
Diane Walker
The story of Jesus feeding more than 5,000 people is beautifully retold in *Jesus and the starving crowd*. It is available in two formats, a big book for group use and a child's reader.
Big Book: £19.99, 1 85999 722 8
Child's reader: £3.50, 1 85999 723 6
Others in the series include:
Jesus and the cheat, Jesus puts things right and *Jesus and the breakfast barbecue*

Children Finding Faith
Francis Bridger
How can we help children know God? In this prize-winning book, Francis Bridger explores how children develop in their faith.
£6.99, 1 85999 323 0

See page 10 for details of Scripture Union's range of booklets for children who want to make a commitment to follow Jesus.

After Awesome!?
Have you tried...

Streetwise
Julie Sharp and Claire Derry
Get streetwise and pop into eight homes that Jesus visited – the cheat's house, the crowded house, the rich man's house – all houses that feature in Luke's Gospel. Another eight-session programme from Scripture Union, aimed at groups that attract children with no church connection. (This programme also works with the *Luke Street* video.)
Resource book: £8.99, 1 85999 767 8
DVD: £14.99, 1 84427 111 0

RESOURCES

Holiday club material

Landlubbers
Paul Wallis
A five-day holiday programme, based on Paul's letter to the Philippians. Children discover the greatest treasure while exploring Paul's story through Philippians and Acts. *Landlubbers Logbook* contains the text of Philippians, together with activies and background information.
Resource book: £8.99, 1 84427 038 6
DVD: £19.99, 1 84427 138 2
Landlubbers Logbook single: £1.99, 1 84427 110 2
Landlubbers Logbook pack of ten: £10.00, 1 84427 112 9
Promotional material and merchandise is available from CPO.

To order these or any of Scripture Union's products, visit your local Christian bookshop or contact SU Mail Order:
Scripture Union Mail Order, PO Box 5148, Milton Keynes MLO, MK2 2YX
Tel: 0845 07 06 006 Fax: 01908 856020
Web: www.scriptureunion.org.uk
Prices correct at time of going to press.

Follow up your holiday club!

Clues2Use
Landlubbers on the Jesus Quest
Jean Elliott
This eight-session programme for midweek clubs is specifically designed to use after you have done a *Landlubbers* hoilday club (although it can stand alone). This programme follows the same pirate theme as *Landlubbers*, helping you keep up the contact with children who have come to your holiday club. In each session, Landlubbers look for Jesus in everyday life. In the supermarket, on the bus, at a football stadium – Landlubbers hear the powerful story of Jesus' death and resurrection, and discover that Jesus is always with them.

Resource book: £8.99 1 84427 113 7
Use with *The Jesus Quest* DVD

eye level clubs...

- are for boys and girls aged 5 to 11.
- are for children who are not yet part of a church (as well as those who are).
- don't assume that children know much about Jesus or have had any experience of church.
- recognise that all children are open to God and the wonder of his world, and that all children can have valid spiritual experiences, regardless of church background.
- aim to give children one of the best hours in their week.
- provide opportunities for appropriate and respectful relationships between children and adults, working in small groups.
- plan to introduce children to the Bible in ways that allow for imagination, exploration and learning difficulties.
- are led by those who long to see children become lifelong followers of Jesus Christ.
- are led by those who will put themselves at a child's level, so that together they can catch sight of Jesus.